SPECTACULAR NORTH DAKOTA HIKES

BRING THE DOG

SUSAN WEFALD

ILLUSTRATIONS BY JANET FLOM

PUBLISHED BY
NORTH DAKOTA INSTITUTE FOR REGIONAL STUDIES
FARGO, NORTH DAKOTA

Published by North Dakota Institute for Regional Studies
North Dakota State University
Dept. 2360 P.O. Box 6050
Fargo, ND 58108-6050
http://www.ndsu.edu/ahss/ndirs/

Spectacular North Dakota Hikes
Bring the dog
written by Susan Wefald.
Copy editing by Catherine Jelsing.
Cover and interior design by Lourdes Hawley.
Cover and interior illustrations by Janet Flom.
Map design by Thomas Marple

ISBN 978-0-911042-75-7
Library of Congress Control Number: 2011932385

Printed in Canada.

Cover Illustration

Pausing to sniff,
Sandy listens
To the distant knocking
Of a woodpecker and
Absorbs the colors of the forest.
                    – Susan Wefald

THANKS TO THE FOLLOWING FOR THEIR HELP WITH THIS BOOK: *Thank you to my husband Bob, who is a great hiking companion and the love of my life. Thank you to my children Sarah, Kate and Tom for their encouragement and support as I hiked and worked on the manuscript.*

Catherine Jelsing, editor; Lourdes Hawley, graphic designer; Thomas Marple, map designer; and Janet Flom, artist, helped me turn my dream of a North Dakota hiking book into reality. I appreciate their dedication, talent, and thoughtfulness. Thank you!

Thank you also to North Dakota Parks and Recreation, North Dakota Forest Service, U.S. Forest Service Dakota Prairie Grasslands, U.S. Department of the Interior Bureau of Land Management and U.S. Fish and Wildlife Service National Wildlife Refuge System for their assistance with the trail maps.

Thank you to Sylvia, my friend and daily walking partner.

CONTENTS

Sharing spectacular hikes with Sandy   *IV*
Plan ahead for a successful hike   *VI*
Spectacular North Dakota Hikes Map   *VIII*

1. MISSOURI RIVER

Area Attractions and Accommodations   **2**
Fort Abraham Lincoln State Park
   Little Soldier Loop Trail   **3**
   Recreation Trail   **6**
Missouri River Natural Area
   Missouri River Natural Area Trail   **7**
Bismarck Parks and Recreation District
   Missouri Valley Legacy Trail   **8**
   Sertoma Riverside Park Zoo Loop   **10**
Double Ditch State Historic Site
   Interpretive Trail   **11**
Cross Ranch State Park
   Upper Loop of the Ma-a-koti Trail   **12**
The Nature Conservancy Cross Ranch Preserve
   Prairie Trail   **15**
Knife River Indian Villages National Historic Site
   Two Rivers Trail   **15**
University of Mary and Annunciation Monastery
   Sageway Path and Labyrinth Walk   **16**
Sibley Nature Park
   Sibley Nature Park Trail   **19**

2. TURTLE MOUNTAINS

Area Attractions and Accommodations   **26**
Lake Metigoshe State Park
   Kings Highway Trail   **27**
   Old Oak Trail   **30**
Butte Saint Paul Historic Site
   Hike to Butte Saint Paul   **31**
International Peace Garden
   Formal Gardens Border Walk   **33**
   Lakeview Hiking Trail   **35**
Turtle Mountain State Forest
   Black Lake Trail in Strawberry Lake Recreation Area   **36**

3. SHEYENNE RIVER VALLEY

Area Attractions and Accommodations **45**
Fort Ransom State Park
 Valley View Trail **46**
 Little Twig Nature Trail **48**
Sheyenne State Forest
 Mineral Springs and Waterfall Trail **49**
 Oak Ridge Hiking Trail **52**
Sheyenne National Grassland
 Hike to Iron Springs **52**

4. LITTLE MISSOURI RIVER BADLANDS

Area Attractions and Accommodations **61**
Theodore Roosevelt National Park — South Unit
 Painted Canyon Trail **62**
 Painted Canyon Nature Trail **66**
Little Missouri State Park
 Bob's Loop **67**
 Travois Trail **70**
Little Missouri National Grassland
 Summit Trail **71**
 Bennett Trail **74**
 Kate's Walk on the Maah Daah Hey Trail **77**
Theodore Roosevelt National Park— North Unit
 Trail to Sperati Point **81**

5. PRAIRIE RIVERS OF THE NORTHEAST

Area Attractions and Accommodations **93**
Turtle River State Park
 Turtle River Forest Loop **94**
Icelandic State Park
 Shady Springs Trail **98**
 Settlers Trail **100**
Greater Grand Forks Greenway
 Downtown Riverfront Walk **101**
University of North Dakota
 Campus Walk **104**

6. LAKE SAKAKAWEA

Area Attractions and Accommodations **111**
Fort Stevenson State Park
    Purple Coneflower Trail **112**
    Flicker Loop Trail **115**
Audubon National Wildlife Refuge
    Prairie Trail **116**
Lake Sakakawea State Park
    Sandy's Loop **117**
Garrison Dam National Fish Hatchery
    Wetlands Observation Trail **120**
Lewis and Clark State Park
    Overlook Trail **121**
Williston Marsh Nature Area
    Recreation Trail **124**

7. CONFLUENCE OF THE MISSOURI & YELLOWSTONE RIVERS

Area Attractions and Accommodations **131**
Sundheim Park Recreation Area
    Fairview Lift Bridge and Cartwright
        Tunnel Trail **132**
Fort Union Trading Post National Historic Site
    Bodmer Overlook Trail **135**
Missouri–Yellowstone Confluence Interpretive Center
    Recreation Trail **138**

8. NATIONAL WILDLIFE REFUGES & OTHER SCENIC LOCATIONS

Area Attractions and Accommodations **144**
Schnell Recreation Area
    Slater Pond and the Bur Oak Nature Trail **145**
Upper Souris National Wildlife Refuge
    Cottonwood Nature Trail **148**
    Oxbow Nature Trail **151**
Des Lacs National Wildlife Refuge
    Munch's Coulee Nature Trail **152**
Lostwood National Wildlife Refuge
    Nature Trail **156**

Hikes at a glance **166**

SHARING SPECTACULAR HIKES WITH SANDY

This book is for anyone who wants to explore North Dakota's diverse landscape and learn more about its history. It's for families who want to expand neighborhood strolls into the great outdoors. It's for seasoned hikers looking for new experiences. And it's for people who love the idea of hiking with their dogs.

On these pages I describe what I consider some of the best day hikes in North Dakota, many of which I've hiked with my dog, Sandy.

Sandy is a 95-pound goldendoodle. I call him my exercise machine. Every day we walk at least two miles together, rain or shine, summer or winter. His pleading eyes and excited prance get me out of the house, even when I'd rather sit on the couch and read a good book. Sandy thinks it's fun walking outdoors when it's 15 below zero.

My husband, Bob, and I have hiked trails all over the United States and in a few foreign countries. As I reflected on those hiking experiences, it occurred to me that many of the hikes I'd taken in North Dakota were just as spectacular as those I'd taken in places better known for hiking. That realization led to the writing of this book.

Breathtaking views, varied ecosystems and interesting historic and cultural sites all contribute to great hikes. While visiting Korea, Bob and I hiked up a hill where ancient peoples had carved images of the Buddha into the rocks. That was a spectacular hike. While North Dakota doesn't have Buddhist relics upon which to gaze, the hikes in this book feature intriguing historic sites and amazing vistas of rivers, prairies, lakes and canyons. Some hikes are in urban areas and some are in remote parts of the state. I've identified 29 spectacular hikes and 21 favorite hikes; each is special in its own way.

Since Bob's schedule often keeps him from accompanying me – and friends aren't always available – Sandy is my companion on many of the hikes described on these pages. With my dog at my side and my cell phone in my pocket, I always feel comfortable and safe on the trail.

Sandy is an enthusiastic hiker. He loves exploring new places. His delight when he finds a painted turtle or sees a pheasant always enhances my hiking experience. I enjoy his calm presence when I sit to enjoy a special flower or view. Sandy is such a big part of the hikes I've included his comments on our adventures. He tells about his encounters with cattle, the importance of steering clear of prickly pear cactus and moments of unexpected fun. Dog owners also will find pertinent advice on hiking with pets in the Plan Ahead for Successful Hikes section.

In each hike description I've included local history, information on the natural environment and practical trail advice. Maps and directions to trailheads are provided for all spectacular hikes. Information on the lengths and elevation change of trails will help you decide whether or not a particular hike is the right one for you. All of the hikes in this book can be completed in one day – many in an hour or so. Motorized vehicles are forbidden on all but one of these trails.

You will notice that What's for lunch? is a part of each hike description. For me eating and hiking go hand in hand. I get hungry when I'm on the trail and adding a picnic to a hike always makes it more memorable. My notes also include suggestions on where to purchase meals, as well as information on area attractions and accommodations.

Please send me your thoughts on these hikes and let me know about other North Dakota day hikes that you love sharing with family, friends and your dog. You may contact me at http://spectacularndhikes.blogspot.com

Happy hiking!

Susan

PLAN AHEAD FOR A SUCCESSFUL HIKE

Be prepared…

- Dress for the weather
- Bring along sufficient water, especially in hot weather
- Dogs need plenty of water; be sure to pack a canvas or plastic bowl
- Wear sturdy shoes
- Wear insect repellent for mosquitoes and ticks
- Check with your veterinarian about tick repellent for your dog
- Hiking sticks can be helpful, especially in the Little Missouri River badlands
- Plan to clean up after your dog along the trail
- Preserve our beautiful places; take only pictures, leave only footprints

CHECK THE DISTANCE

I have indicated the length of each hike. When a hike is labeled round trip the hike is to a destination and you will return to the trailhead via the same path. The length of each round-trip hike is the total length of hiking both directions. The length of a loop hike is the total distance of the loop.

STEER CLEAR OF HUNTERS

Hunting is popular in North Dakota and some hikes in this book are in locations where hunting is allowed. I have labeled these hikes with hunting alerts and do not recommend hiking these trails during hunting seasons. North Dakota hunting seasons begin in early September and extend through mid-May. Consult North Dakota Game and Fish regarding hunting calendars, 701.328.6300 or http://gf.nd.gov.

STAY ALERT IN BADLANDS

I have hiked the Little Missouri River badlands for more than 30 years and have always had wonderful, safe adventures, but hikers must take a few precautions.

- Do not hike badlands trails if it has recently rained or if wet weather is approaching. Ridges and trails in the badlands contain bentonite clay, which becomes extremely slippery when wet, creating dangerous trail conditions. When dry, the light grey clay resembles popped corn and presents no trail difficulties.
- In hot summer months, hike badlands trails in the morning or evening.
- Bison are dangerous. Take a wide detour around bison if you see them on a hike. Bison are found only in Theodore Roosevelt National Park and the Nature Conservancy Cross Ranch Preserve.
- Adequate water is extremely important for you and your dog.

IN WINTER, CALL AHEAD

The hiking season in North Dakota generally runs from mid-April to early November. Some of the trails in this book are not maintained in the winter, but if snowfall is light they may be passable. Call ahead for information on winter trail conditions.

TELL OTHERS YOUR DESTINATION

When hiking, it's important to tell others where you are going and when to expect your return.

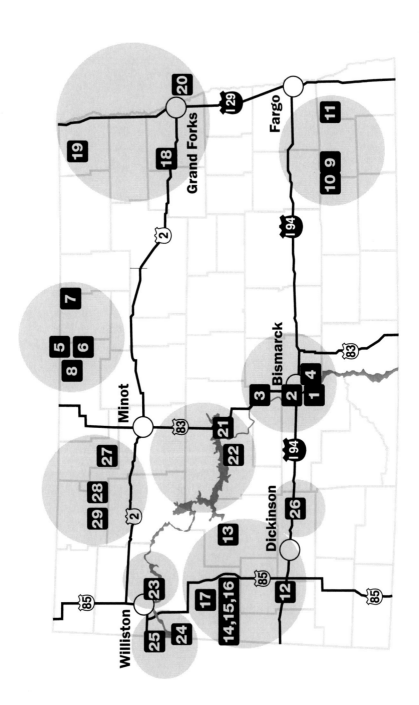

MISSOURI RIVER

1 Little Soldier Loop Trail
2 Missouri Valley Legacy Trail
3 Upper Loop of the Ma-a-koti Trail
4 Sageway Path and Labyrinth Walk

TURTLE MOUNTAINS

5 Kings Highway Trail
6 Hike to Butte Saint Paul
7 Formal Gardens Border Walk
8 Black Lake Trail

SHEYENNE RIVER VALLEY

9 Valley View Trail
10 Mineral Springs and Waterfall Trail
11 Hike to Iron Springs

LITTLE MISSOURI RIVER BADLANDS

12 Painted Canyon Trail
13 Bob's Loop
14 Summit Trail
15 Bennett Trail
16 Kate's Walk on the Maah Daah Hey Trail
17 Trail to Sperati Point

PRAIRIE RIVERS OF THE NORTHEAST

18 Turtle River Forest Loop
19 Shady Springs Trail
20 Downtown Riverfront Walk

LAKE SAKAKAWEA

21 Purple Coneflower Trail
22 Sandy's Loop
23 Overlook Trail

CONFLUENCE OF THE MISSOURI AND YELLOWSTONE RIVERS

24 Fairview Lift Bridge and Cartwright Tunnel Trail
25 Bodmer Overlook Trail

NATIONAL WILDLIFE REFUGES & OTHER SCENIC LOCATIONS

26 Slater Pond and the Bur Oak Nature Trail
27 Cottonwood Nature Trail
28 Munch's Coulee Nature Trail
29 Nature Trail (Lostwood)

On a gorgeous
Blue and gold autumn day
The shadows of the past
Accompany me on my hike.
— Susan Wefald

AREA ATTRACTIONS

Fort Abraham Lincoln State Park is a great place for history buffs and lovers of the outdoors. Tour On-a-Slant Indian Village, with six reconstructed Mandan earth lodges, and explore a fascinating frontier fort. Partially reconstructed Fort Abraham Lincoln, home of the 7th Cavalry, features three blockhouses and the house from which General George Custer left to fight the Battle of the Little Big Horn. The park visitor center and museum also have excellent exhibits.

WHERE TO HIKE

- *Fort Abraham Lincoln State Park, Mandan*
- *Missouri River Natural Area, Mandan*
- *Bismarck Parks and Recreation District, Bismarck*
- *Double Ditch State Historic Site, Bismarck*
- *Cross Ranch State Park, Washburn*
- *The Nature Conservancy Cross Ranch Preserve, Washburn*
- *Knife River Indian Villages National Historic Site, Stanton*
- *University of Mary and Annunciation Monastery, Bismarck*
- *Sibley Nature Park, Bismarck*

~ Sertoma Riverside Park in Bismarck includes an amusement park with Ferris wheel, merry-go-round, miniature golf and other amusements. The Dakota Zoo also is located here.

~ Riverboat Rides on the Missouri River are available at The Port of Bismarck.

~ The North Dakota State Capitol Building and neighboring North Dakota Heritage Center are must-sees in Bismarck. Built in the 1930s, the art deco capitol building often is referred to as the skyscraper of the prairie. Walking paths on the capitol's extensive grounds connect sculptures, memorials, an arboretum and seasonal flower gardens.

~ North Dakota Lewis and Clark Interpretive Center and Fort Mandan Historic Site are located just north of Washburn. The Corps of Discovery built Fort Mandan and wintered there in 1804-1805. Both sites have outstanding exhibits.

~ Falkirk Mine, north of Washburn, offers tours of its open-pit coal mining and reclamation operation.

❧ Canoe the Missouri River using the canoe service at Cross Ranch State Park.

❧ Knife River Indian Villages National Historic Site, 25 miles west of Washburn, features a reconstructed earth lodge, museum and historic earth lodge village sites.

AREA ACCOMMODATIONS

❧ Fort Abraham Lincoln State Park offers large shady campgrounds on the Missouri River.

❧ General Sibley Park, 5 miles south of Bismarck, has a large shady campground near the Missouri River.

❧ Cross Ranch State Park has three primitive cabins and two yurts for rent. Charming and comfortable, the cabins are set back from the Missouri River among tall cottonwood trees. The park also has a shady campground.

❧ The cities of Mandan and Bismarck provide many lodging options.

❧ Washburn has RV parks and motel accommodations.

FORT ABRAHAM LINCOLN STATE PARK
LITTLE SOLDIER LOOP TRAIL

What makes this hike spectacular? **Little Soldier Loop Trail is on high prairie bluffs along the western edge of the Missouri River. Outstanding views of the river valley make this trail one of the most scenic in the state. Sights along the trail include a reconstructed Mandan Indian village, infantry post blockhouses and a cavalry post on the plain below. In the distance, the North Dakota State Capitol building looms over the city of Bismarck.**

AT A GLANCE
LITTLE SOLDIER LOOP TRAIL

Map:	**Page 20**
Location:	**Fort Abraham Lincoln State Park**
Nearest town:	**Mandan**
Length:	**2.1-mile loop**
Elevation change:	**140 feet**
Dogs:	**Allowed on leashes**
Fees:	**Park entrance fee**
Services at trailhead:	**Trail map, picnic area and vault toilet**

DIRECTIONS TO TRAILHEAD

Fort Abraham Lincoln State Park is 7 miles south of Mandan on Highway 1806. After you enter the park, proceed 1 mile north on the main park road. Turn left when you reach the road to the infantry post. You will see a picnic area and the trailhead on your right.

SUSAN'S NOTES ON THE HIKE

This trail – one of my favorite short hikes in the state – celebrates the role Army scouts played in this area during the 1870s. As you hike, you'll feel like a scout too.

To enjoy the best views of the Missouri River Valley, be sure to follow the directional arrows on the trail map. The first 0.35-mile section of the trail is part of Young Hawk Interpretive Loop. It heads west and then turns east as it heads up the hill toward Fort Abraham Lincoln infantry post. At the top of the hill you join Little Soldier Loop Trail, which leads north, past one of the fort's three blockhouses.

The Army built an infantry post on a bluff overlooking the confluence of the Missouri and Heart rivers in 1872 to protect railroad workers laying tracks to the West. Almost as soon as the infantry post was completed, the Army realized in order to carry out its mission it needed cavalry. So, in 1873 the Army established a cavalry post down the hill, near the river. Fort Abraham Lincoln was now ready for action.

I love climbing the steps of the infantry blockhouse, about 0.5 mile from the trailhead. North of the blockhouse the trail weaves through native prairie near woody draws filled with bur oak and green ash and other hardwoods.

You can expand this 2.1-mile hike into a 3.6-mile hike by adding Little Sioux Loop and Bob-Tailed Bull Pass; you'll find the sign about 1 mile into the hike. If you add these loops, be sure you return to this point and rejoin Little Soldier Loop so you don't miss the lovely views.

For the 2.1-mile version of the hike, continue north on Little Soldier Trail as it meanders along a prairie ridge. The trail turns east and then follows the top of the bluff south for approximately 1 mile. Vistas of the Missouri River Valley along this portion of the trail make this hike truly memorable. The North Dakota State Capitol stands tall over the city of Bismarck to your east. There are also nice views of the confluence of the Heart and Missouri rivers. As you near the end of the trail, On-A-Slant Mandan Indian Village stretches below you. An active village from 1575 to 1781, many earth lodges once were located here; six have been rebuilt as part of Fort Abraham Lincoln State Park Museum.

Sandy and I have seen ring-necked pheasants, hawks, bald eagles and western meadowlarks along the trail. We love looking at the yucca lilies, which grow in native prairie areas all the way from North Dakota down into Texas. One day in mid April we spotted hundreds of pasque flowers, also known as prairie crocuses. Pale purple coneflowers bloom in July and August. While the trail mainly travels through native prairie, wildflowers were planted in areas disturbed when the trail was built in 2007.

SANDY'S NOTES ON THE HIKE

Plains prickly pear cacti grow in the native prairie along the trail, so I stay on the path.

WHAT'S FOR LUNCH?

A visit to Fort Abraham Lincoln State Park isn't complete without a picnic cook-out. The Civilian Conservation Corps picnic ground at Little Soldier Loop trailhead is nice, but Sandy and I prefer the rustic stone picnic shelter 0.5 mile north of the trailhead. Also constructed by the CCC, this shelter has a fireplace and picnic table and provides lovely views of the Missouri River Valley. You can walk or drive to this shaded picnic spot. For an October picnic with a young friend from Russia, Bob and I grilled hot dogs on sticks and warmed a can of baked beans in the coals of the fire. We rounded out the meal with hotdog buns, carrot sticks, potato chips, apples, apple cider and fudge brownies.

OTHER FAVORITE HIKES

FORT ABRAHAM LINCOLN STATE PARK
RECREATION TRAIL (2 MILES)

This recreation trail follows an old state park entrance road. Hiking north you'll see the confluence of the Heart and Missouri rivers and surrounding countryside. On your return, you'll have excellent views of the Huff Hills along the Missouri River to the south.

This 2-mile, round-trip hike starts in the same place as Little Soldier Loop trailhead (see above). Take the paved trail north, overlooking the earth lodges of the Mandan Indian Village, and continue walking 1 mile until you reach the unmanned entrance to the state park. Leashed dogs are allowed.

Keep an eye on the sky for hawks, bald eagles and turkey vultures. In the spring, migrating geese gather by the thousands in grain fields along the Missouri River. One day in March, Bob and I saw 10 bald eagles circling high in the sky, ready to prey on geese in the fields below.

MISSOURI RIVER NATURAL AREA TRAIL (5.5 MILES)

The Missouri River Natural Area Trail, just north of Mandan, follows the wooded banks of the Missouri River for 2 miles, crosses under I-94 and loops through 1.5 miles of cottonwood forest along a river bay. The only drawback to this level, scenic hike is that in some places it passes within 500 feet of I-94 and you hear the noise of passing highway traffic. That being said, this is a pleasant 5.5-mile loop hike. Numerous places along the trail provide access the riverbank, which makes it a great place for fishing.

To access the trailhead: Take I-94 to Exit 133 and turn south under I-94 (Mandan Avenue). Immediately south of I-94, turn onto Division Street Northeast and as soon as you cross the railroad tracks, turn north onto River Drive Northeast. You will drive under I-94 again and then turn left on the first road. The trailhead is 0.5 mile down this road. A map is posted at the trailhead. Leashed dogs are allowed.

Even a short hike along this trail is memorable. I've hiked here in the springtime and watched huge ice chunks float downriver. In the fall I've enjoyed seeing the beautiful gold leaves of eastern cottonwood trees. Every season offers a new experience.

QUESTIONS?

~ Fort Abraham Lincoln State Park, 701.667.6340, www.parkrec.nd.gov/parks/flsp.htm

BISMARCK PARKS AND RECREATION DISTRICT

MISSOURI VALLEY LEGACY TRAIL

What makes this hike spectacular? **Bismarck Parks and Recreation District maintains many miles of recreation trails and this hike includes some of the most scenic segments of the city's trail system. In the 1870s this part of Bismarck was a busy port, with steamboats providing transportation where railroad service ended, taking people and freight further west. On this hike you will explore four distinct areas: The Missouri River's sandy shoreline; Keelboat Park, with its boating facilities and historical exhibits; shady Pioneer Park; and the Missouri River bluffs, where you'll find Chief Looking's Village and a terrific view of the river.**

AT A GLANCE

MISSOURI VALLEY LEGACY TRAIL

Map:	**Page 21**
Trail location:	**Bismarck Parks and Recreation District**
Nearest town:	**Bismarck**
Length:	**3.7 miles round trip**
Elevation change:	**155 feet**
Dogs:	**Allowed on leashes**
Fees:	**None**
Services at trailhead:	**None**

DIRECTIONS TO TRAILHEAD

This hike starts in Steamboat Park on Riverside Park Road, 0.5-mile north of Missouri River Memorial Bridge, across from the Bismarck City Water Treatment Plant. A series of eagle sculptures created by student artists at United Tribes Technical College are in place along the trail. A pamphlet describing the sculptures is available from Bismarck Parks and Recreation District.

SUSAN'S NOTES ON THE HIKE

Missouri Valley Legacy Trail is frequented by walkers, cyclists and inline skaters. The paved trail runs north and south of Steamboat Park along Riverside Park Road. There's a lot to see along the first section of the trail, beginning with Yellowstone Steamboat, a 60-foot-long replica of steamboats that plied these waters from the 1830s into the early 20th century.

Sandy and I enjoy looking at Reflections, one of the eagle sculptures created by Native American student artists. We often scramble down the riverbank to wade along the narrow, sand beaches. And we always hope to see a train on the Burlington Northern Santa Fe railroad bridge. Built in 1882, it's the only North Dakota railroad bridge that crosses the Missouri River.

Watch out for traffic as the trail enters Keelboat Park. Lewis & Clark Riverboat docks here – at the Port of Bismarck – between cruises. You'll also find a Lewis and Clark historical exhibit, a second eagle sculpture titled Thunderbirds and public lavatories.

The trail continues north through Pioneer Park, past a river marsh and beneath majestic eastern cottonwood trees. You'll see a third eagle sculpture, Rising Eagle, near the far north end of the park. Just beyond this point, at the traffic intersection, the trail crosses River Road. Proceed uphill through grasslands and small woody draws and – just before you reach the top of the hill – turn left onto the grassy path to Chief Looking's Village. You will want to visit this site.

Mandan Indians lived in Chief Looking's Village between 1675 and 1780. None of the Mandan earth lodges remain, but you can capture the spirit of the place by walking through the site. Interpretive signs along the short path provide insight into village life. Look for the large stone on the north side of the site that was used both for washing clothes and for grinding corn. On the west edge of the village there's an outstanding vantage point of the Missouri River Valley.

From here, there are two ways to return to your starting point. One option is to turn around and go back the way you came. The other option (the one Sandy and I prefer) is a more adventurous route and 0.75- mile shorter. Begin by retracing your steps until you see a dirt path near a culvert, about 200 feet below the end of the paved walking trail. Take this path south. The trail winds through wooded areas and along grassy, west-facing river bluffs. You will see a number of dirt paths, but continue heading south and downhill. You will rejoin the paved trail when you cross River Road under Highway I-94.

SANDY'S NOTES ON THE HIKE

I like the drinking fountain for dogs at the Port of Bismarck. Look for it near the Lewis and Clark historical exhibit. Sometimes Susan lets me cool off in the river, but she won't let me go in too deep due to the current.

WHAT'S FOR LUNCH?

If you bring along a picnic lunch, Pioneer Park offers lots of picnic tables. The ticket office at the Port of Bismarck sells snacks and soft drinks. Hours of operation are seasonal.

OTHER FAVORITE HIKES

SERTOMA RIVERSIDE PARK
ZOO LOOP (1.7 MILES)

On the Zoo Loop through Bismarck's Sertoma Riverside Park you'll experience Missouri River wetlands, hike the perimeter of Dakota Zoo and you can visit a small amusement park.

Sertoma Riverside Park is on Riverside Park Road, 0.5-mile south of Memorial Bridge. Follow signs to Shelter 5 and park your vehicle; the hike starts and ends here. Leashed dogs are allowed.

Directly across the access road from Shelter 5 a well-worn dirt trail heads west toward the river. Follow it to the paved walking path. Turn left (south) on the paved path. I have seen ducks, geese, skunks, white-tailed deer and beaver in the river wetlands adjacent to the trail. Many species of birds also frequent the area.

When you come to the underpass, turn left (east) and proceed along the south side of the zoo. Within 0.25 mile, you'll see camels in a pasture on your left. When you reach the first path by the base-ball diamonds, turn left (north). The trail soon passes tennis courts and huge eastern cottonwood trees. Near the zoo entrance, look to your right to see Gathering of Visions, an eagle sculpture created by local Native American student artists.

Continue walking north along the zoo fence toward Shelter 5. Along the way you will pass more zoo animals – including aoudad and llamas – and a small amusement park. In summer I enjoy riding the Ferris wheel and grabbing a snack at the nearby community center.

DOUBLE DITCH STATE HISTORIC SITE
INTERPRETIVE TRAIL (0.75 MILE)

Double Ditch State Historic Site preserves the remains of a Mandan village. Built high above the Missouri River on an ancient river terrace, the village was occupied by Mandan Indians from 1490 to 1785. In the 1930s the Civilian Conservation Corps built a stone shelter here. In addition to offering glimpses of the past, the trail offers wonderful vistas of the Missouri River and surrounding countryside.

The entrance to the site is 8 miles north of Bismarck on Highway 1804. The trailhead is adjacent to the parking lot. The level, loop trail circles the village. Interpretive signs provide information from historical records and archeological studies. Leashed dogs are allowed.

Adjacent to the historic site is Double Ditch State Recreation Area. The riverside recreation area offers a 1-mile, round-trip recreation trail, picnic tables and interpretive information. Keep your eye on children and pets in the picnic area as there are steep cliffs along the river.

QUESTIONS?

~ Bismarck Parks and Recreation District, 701.222.6455; www.bisparks.org

~ State Historical Society of North Dakota, 701.328.2666, www.nd.gov/hist

CROSS RANCH STATE PARK

CROSS RANCH STATE PARK
UPPER LOOP OF THE MA-A-KOTI TRAIL

What makes this hike spectacular? **Exploring this trail will make you feel like a member of Lewis and Clark's Corps of Discovery. The famed explorers may have walked these same grounds 200 years ago. The views of the countryside along the river are outstanding, plus the hike features three distinct plant environments: a river valley forest, an ancient river terrace and the river shoreline.**

AT A GLANCE

UPPER LOOP OF THE MA-A-KOTI TRAIL

Map:	**Page 22**
Location:	**Cross Ranch State Park**
Nearest town:	**Washburn**
Length:	**2.5-mile loop**
Elevation change:	**Less than 50 feet**
Dogs:	**Allowed on leashes**
Fees:	**State park entrance fee**
Services at trailhead:	**Visitor center, lavatory, trail map**

DIRECTIONS TO TRAILHEAD

Cross Ranch State Park is 12 miles southwest of Washburn on Highway 1806. To the right of the visitor center there's a parking lot. Nearby you'll see the Matah Trail trailhead. The hike starts here and then joins the upper loop of the Ma-a-koti Trail.

SUSAN'S NOTES ON THE HIKE

A favorite trail of ours for years, Bob and I hike here spring, summer and fall. We always have interesting experiences and appreciate the terrific views.

The first 0.5 mile of the hike is on the Matah Trail. The well-marked, paved trail soon turns into a grassy pathway through a river-bottom forest filled with eastern cottonwood trees. This path leads to the start of Ma-a-koti Trail, which briefly follows the river. A stairway leads upward to an ancient river terrace covered by native prairie grasses. Thousands of years ago, when the Missouri River carried meltwater from the glaciers, this area was a river floodplain.

Captains Lewis and Clark traveled through North Dakota on the Missouri River in 1804, 1805 and 1806. As they traveled up the river, expedition members often explored the surrounding countryside on foot, sometimes accompanied by Lewis' dog Seaman. The fall of 1804 the Corps of Discovery built a small fort on the riverbank and spent the winter near what is now the town of Washburn. Before departing for the Pacific Ocean in the spring of 1805, the corps filled a boat with a huge shipment – including specimens of native flora, fauna and minerals – and sent it to Washington, D.C.

The last time Bob, Sandy and I took this hike the prairie berry plants were thick with fruit. We saw buffalo berry bushes with red berries and chokecherry bushes hanging low with black cherries. Even the woodbine vines were laden with yellow berries.

After you've hiked up and down several small dips in the prairie, you'll reach the high point of the trail. We like sitting here to rest and enjoy the scents and sights of the prairie. In August, a purple blazing star (or liatris) standing in the prairie grass reminded us not all late-blooming wildflowers are yellow. Looking south, we gazed on the majestic buttes along the Missouri River. Looking west, we viewed the open ranchland. Just as we were preparing to move on, a bald eagle flew within 100 feet of our perch. As we watched it fly south along the river valley, two small birds attacked it. Now that was a special moment.

Continuing on Ma-a-koti Trail, you'll come to a bridge over a ravine where the trail veers toward the river. (For a scenic side trip that will add 3 miles to your hike, cross the bridge and proceed 1.5 miles to Senger Boat Ramp.) I always look forward to the river section of the hike, where green ash, eastern cottonwood and willow trees thrive along a not-so-lazy Missouri. Sandy and I love wading in the shallows, but caution is required as the current is strong just a few feet from shore. I enjoy scavenging the narrow beach for interesting pieces of driftwood.

To return to the trailhead, continue north on the Ma-a-koti Trail and rejoin the Matah Trail.

WHAT'S FOR LUNCH?

On a cool August afternoon when Bob joined Sandy and me on this hike, the high temperature was only 64 so we felt like eating a hot meal. We brought along our camp stove and I planned a menu with two pots in mind. In one skillet I browned thin-cut pork chops, sautéed some onions, then added a small can of sauerkraut (and a little beer for flavor). In the other pot I heated pre-made German potato salad. Sliced, homegrown tomatoes and a dessert of cheese kuken completed our delicious picnic supper.

Cross Ranch has several picnic spots. Our favorite is in the group campground, because it's right on the river and it's protected from wind and sun by large trees. The closest place to pick up picnic supplies or purchase lunch is Washburn, 12 miles north of the park.

SANDY'S NOTES ON THE HIKE

My favorite part of this hike is splashing in the river, but I also love all the smells of the prairie.

OTHER FAVORITE HIKES

THE NATURE CONSERVANCY CROSS RANCH PRESERVE
PRAIRIE TRAIL (2 MILES)

For an excellent prairie hike on native upland prairie, with outstanding views of the Missouri River, I recommend Cross Ranch Preserve Prairie Trail. Adjacent to Cross Ranch State Park, The Nature Conservancy's 5,593-acre preserve is home to bison, beautiful wildflowers and many species of birds.

A trailhead for the 2-mile loop trail is located across from the main entrance to Cross Ranch State Park. A map and brochures are available here. Enter the fenced preserve through the large gate. Since there are few trees on the native prairie, in hot weather it's best to hike in the morning or evening. **Dogs are not allowed on the preserve.**

I love climbing the gentle prairie bluffs with the prairie all around me. About 0.33 mile into the hike you'll come upon a small graveyard where the ranch's previous owners are buried. Views of the Missouri River Valley are superb from this vantage point.

When my friend Sylvia and I hiked here we spotted bison grazing in the distance. We also hiked past a bison wallow and found bison droppings along the trail. In this pastoral setting the bison may appear docile, but they can be extremely dangerous. If you see bison on the trail, take a wide detour around them.

KNIFE RIVER INDIAN VILLAGES NATIONAL HISTORIC SITE
TWO RIVERS TRAIL (6.5 MILES)

Native Americans lived in earthlodge villages on this site for about 500 years. It was here, at the confluence of the Knife and Missouri rivers, that explorers Lewis and Clark met their Shoshone-Hidatsa guide, Sakakawea. Two Rivers Trail is one of three hiking trails at Knife River Indian Villages National Historic Site. It winds for 3.25 miles between the Knife and Missouri rivers – past farm fields and through light forest – to the confluence of the two rivers.

You can get a trail map and historical information at the historic site visitor center, 0.5 mile north of Stanton on County Road 37. To find the Two Rivers Trail trailhead, drive north on the road in front of the visitor center. Just after Knife River Bridge turn right and follow the signs. A map for this level, round-trip trail is posted at the trailhead. Leashed dogs are allowed.

QUESTIONS?

~ Cross Ranch State Park, 701.794.3731, www.parkrec.nd.gov/parks/crsp.htm

~ The Nature Conservancy Cross Ranch Preserve, 701.794.8741, www.nature.org

~ Knife River Indian Villages National Historic Site, 701.745.3300; www.nps.gov/knri

THE UNIVERSITY OF MARY & ANNUNCIATION MONASTERY
SAGEWAY PATH
AND LABYRINTH WALK

W*hat makes this hike spectacular?* **Built on bluffs overlooking the Missouri River, the University of Mary campus is a gem of modern architecture on the prairie. The university's Sageway Path and Annunciation Monastery's Labyrinth Walk offer wonderful views of the valley below. Since the labyrinth is a sacred place, the monastery requests that those walking it maintain the peace and quiet and respect the prayerful atmosphere. The labyrinth is not appropriate for dogs.**

AT A GLANCE

SAGEWAY PATH AND LABYRINTH WALK

Map:	**Page 23**
Location:	**University of Mary and Annunciation Monastery**
Length:	**1.4 miles round trip**
Elevation change:	**Less than 50 feet**
Dogs:	**Allowed on leashes on Sageway Path. No dogs at the Labyrinth.**
Fees:	**None**
Services at trailhead:	**Information desk, lavatories**

DIRECTIONS TO TRAILHEAD

The University of Mary is 4 miles south of Bismarck Airport on University Drive (Highway 1804). Enter the University of Mary campus at the north entrance and park in the large parking lot, just south of the tennis courts. The hike starts at the steps between Clairmont Center and Casey Center. You'll find an information desk and lavatories inside the Casey Center.

SUSAN'S NOTES ON THE HIKE

Summer evenings are a perfect time to hike Sageway Path, but even with snow on the ground, this was an exceptional hike on the sunny March afternoon Sandy and I walked it.

The Benedictine Sisters who established the University of Mary – the state's only private Catholic university – came to Dakota Territory in 1878. Their prayerful and active presence has enhanced the Bismarck community ever since.

Start the hike by walking up the steps adjacent to the Casey Center. Proceed through the outdoor hallway that frames a fine view of the Missouri River. Sageway Path begins on an escarpment over-looking the river. You can see for miles in many directions. Note the broad turns the Missouri River makes through the floodplain. In North Dakota, the Missouri is free flowing for only 100 miles. Most of its waters are controlled via a system of lakes and dams. From this spot you can view one of the most beautiful stretches of the free-flowing river.

Walk south on the path through campus, noting the architecture of the buildings. All were built to capture views of the river and five were designed by noted architect Marcel Breuer. In the distance you will see the Breuer-designed University of Mary Bell Tower. The tower base is the next viewing point on the hike. To reach it, follow the path to the east side of Boniface Hall, next to a park-ing lot. Walk to the tower base and look to the southeast for more beautiful views of the Missouri.

At this point, if you wish to take the Labyrinth Walk, walk down the road leading southeast. Within 0.12 mile you will see the laby-rinth on a stretch of upland prairie. Information brochures can be found in the birdhouse-like structure at the start of the walk.

According to the Sisters of the Annunciation Monastery brochure, the tradition of labyrinths or prayer paths dates back more than 5,000 years. This stone-edged path through the prairie was dedi-cated in 2003. Visitors of all faiths and ages are welcome to use the labyrinth between 8 a.m. and 9 p.m. The monastery's hospitality center offers sessions on using the labyrinth. It is a beautiful, peace-ful place to walk and meditate.

To return to your car, retrace your steps or take the walkway through the middle of campus.

SANDY'S NOTES ON THE HIKE

I love seeing some of the 2,800 students who attend the University of Mary. Inevitably, someone wants to pet me.

WHAT'S FOR LUNCH?

This is such a short hike, usually even I don't get hungry. Maybe it's because this hike provides so much food for the spirit. If your stomach is growling, and classes are in session, visitors are welcome to purchase meals in University Hall cafeteria. You'll also find numerous restaurants in Bismarck.

ANOTHER FAVORITE HIKE

SIBLEY NATURE PARK TRAIL (1 MILE)

Sibley Nature Park is in the Missouri River bottomlands, right below the University of Mary campus. This loop trail meanders through an old cottonwood forest and follows the riverbank for about 0.25 mile, offering great views of a wide bend in the river.

To reach the trailhead, take University Way south to 48th Street. Turn west on 48th Street and drive .5 to Sibley Drive and turn south. Just over 2 miles south (along Apple Creek), turn west on Dogwood Drive and proceed west to the trailhead parking lot. A trail map is posted at the trailhead. Leashed dogs are allowed.

This is an excellent spot for bird watching. One August morning I spotted a brown thrasher, several yellow-shafted flickers, a black-capped chickadee and robins.

QUESTIONS?

~ The University of Mary, 701.255.7500, www.umary.edu

~ Benedictine Sisters of Annunciation Monastery, 701.255.1520, www.annunciationmonastery.org

To enjoy the best views of the Missouri River Valley, be sure to follow the directional arrows on the trail map.

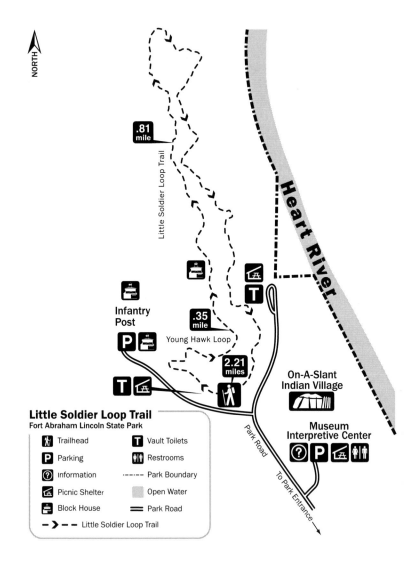

Want to know more about this trail?

TURN TO PAGE 3

Look for the large stone on the north side of Chief Looking's Village that was used both for washing clothes and for grinding corn.

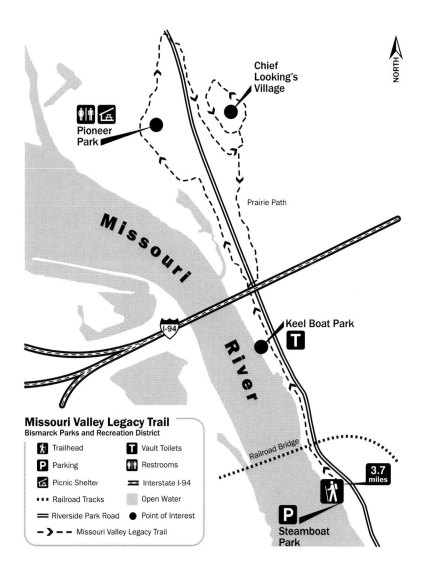

Want to know more about this trail?

TURN TO PAGE 8

I always look forward to the river section of the hike, where green ash, eastern cottonwood and willow trees thrive along a not-so-lazy Missouri.

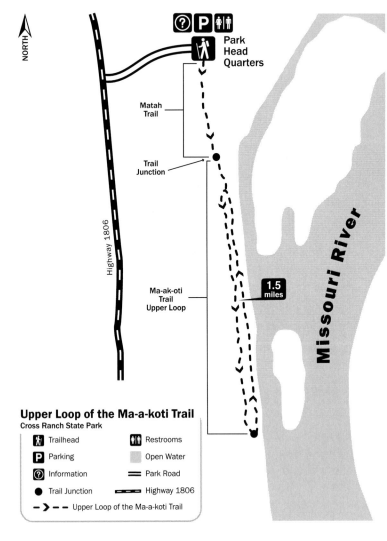

Upper Loop of the Ma-a-koti Trail
Cross Ranch State Park

🚶 Trailhead	🚻 Restrooms
🅿 Parking	▨ Open Water
❓ Information	▬ Park Road
● Trail Junction	▭▭ Highway 1806
➤ - - Upper Loop of the Ma-a-koti Trail	

Want to know more about this trail?
TURN TO PAGE 12

Note the broad turns the Missouri River makes through the floodplain.
In North Dakota, the Missouri is free flowing for only 100 miles.

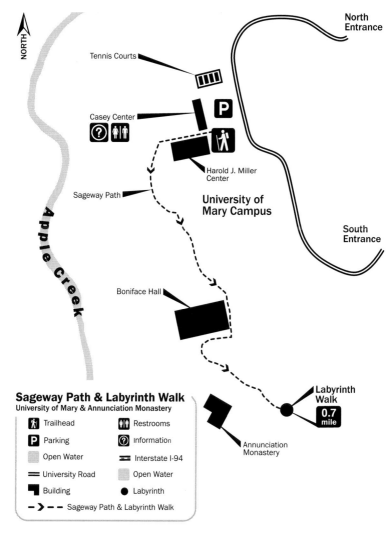

North
Entrance

NORTH

Tennis Courts

Casey Center

P

Harold J. Miller
Center

Sageway Path

University of
Mary Campus

South
Entrance

Apple Creek

Boniface Hall

Labyrinth
Walk
0.7
mile

Sageway Path & Labyrinth Walk
University of Mary & Annunciation Monastery

	Trailhead		Restrooms
P	Parking		Information
	Open Water		Interstate I-94
	University Road		Open Water
	Building	●	Labyrinth
- > - -	Sageway Path & Labyrinth Walk		

Annunciation
Monastery

Want to know more about this trail?
TURN TO PAGE 16

MY NOTES

- TWO -
TURTLE MOUNTAINS

The Turtle Mountains call me
When I crave rolling hills,
Woodsy trails, swimming beaches and
Colorful gardens.
                              — Susan Wefald

AREA ATTRACTIONS

Lake Metigoshe State Park features a large, sandy swimming beach and boat launch facilities. The park rents canoes and cross-country ski equipment.

WHERE TO HIKE

- *Lake Metigoshe State Park, Bottineau*
- *Butte Saint Paul Historic Site, Bottineau*
- *International Peace Garden, Dunseith*
- *Turtle Mountain State Forest, Bottineau*

～ Lake Metigoshe is a beautiful lake in the Turtle Mountains. Surrounded by cabins, the popular lake features great boating and fishing.

～ Butte Saint Paul Historic Site provides a grand view over the plains south of the Turtle Mountains.

～ International Peace Garden spans 2,300 acres in Canada and the United States. Attractions include beautiful flower gardens, monuments, exhibits, summer music programs, Game Warden Museum and a conservatory.

～ Turtle Mountain Chippewa Heritage Center and Turtle Mountain Tribal Arts Gallery in Belcourt display Turtle Mountain Chippewa art and history.

～ Strawberry Lake Recreation Area in Turtle Mountain State Forest lures visitors with hiking trails, a sandy swimming beach, picnic and boat launch areas.

～ Mystical Horizons, North Dakota's Stonehenge for the 21st Century, is made of stone and concrete structures designed for viewing the summer and winter solstices and equinox. The site also has a sundial and a tube for viewing the North Star and offers grand views of the prairie west of the Turtle Mountains. It's located 1 mile west of Strawberry Lake Recreation Area.

AREA ACCOMMODATIONS

～ Lake Metigoshe State Park has a large, shady campground and five cabins for rent. This is a popular resort area and other accommodations can be found nearby.

~   Turtle Mountain State Forest offers campgrounds, including primitive camping sites at Strawberry Lake Recreation Area.

~   International Peace Garden has a large campground on the U.S. side of the park.

~   Belcourt, Dunseith and Bottineau offer lodging.

LAKE METIGOSHE STATE PARK

KINGS HIGHWAY TRAIL

What makes this hike spectacular? **The forested, hilly area along the Canadian border known as the Turtle Mountains was once frequented by English fur trappers. The trails and canoe routes the trappers followed were known as the Kings Highway. Follow their footsteps on this hike through grassy meadows and diverse aspen forests to backcountry lakes where industrious beavers build their lodges. This section of Kings Highway Trail starts less than 0.5 mile south of the Canadian border and leads to a bridge between Eramosh and Rost lakes.**

AT A GLANCE

KINGS HIGHWAY TRAIL

Map:	**Page 39**
Location:	**Lake Metigoshe State Park**
Nearest town:	**Bottineau**
Length:	**3 miles round trip or 1 mile round trip to Eramosh Lake**
Elevation change:	**Less than 50 feet**
Dogs:	**Allowed on leashes**
Fees:	**Park entrance fee**
Services at trailhead:	**Map of trail system**

DIRECTIONS TO TRAILHEAD

Lake Metigoshe State Park is 14 miles northeast of Bottineau. The well-marked trailhead is on the main park road, 1.2 miles north of the entrance station.

SUSAN'S NOTES ON THE HIKE

Sandy and I sensed that we were way up north when we started our hike on Kings Highway Trail. We passed through an open, sunny grove of quaking aspen and enjoyed bird songs and wildflowers in a stretch of meadow. Across the meadow a small backcountry pond sparkled in the sunshine. And, as we walked near School Section Lake and two more ponds, we spotted a beaver lodge.

Soon we entered a dark, dense pine forest filled with the holiday smell of pine needles. The short side trail to Eramosh Lake is 0.5 mile from the start of the hike. Turn left (north) to find the lake, which is surrounded by forest.

Eramosh Lake is a beautiful, rather large lake that straddles the U.S.-Canada border. On the warm, early-August morning Sandy and I hiked here, I removed my shoes, waded into the cool water and lingered for awhile on the narrow gravel beach.

Although the next section of trail is near the south shore of Lake Eramosh, tree foliage blocks the lake from view. The forest here is dominated by quaking aspen, which is easily mistaken for birch because of its bark's light color. Paper birch does grow here, along with bur oak, box elder and green ash.

Young aspen forests offer excellent wildlife habitat and food for deer and moose. Beaver love chewing on aspen because it's easy to cut and the outer tissue provides good nutrition. In new-growth forests, young ruffed grouse eat aspen leaves, leaf buds and flower buds and other plants. Historically, wildfires burned down the old trees – aspens live 60 to 80 years – allowing younger trees to grow. However, the last huge wildfire came through the Turtle Mountains in the late 1800s, so park officials create a mix of aspen stands by cutting some areas and allowing the aspen to re-sprout.

As you continue hiking east down the trail, you'll glimpse marshy Rost Lake through the trees and then see the bridge between Eramosh and Rost lakes. The sun shining on Eramosh Lake and surrounding woods created a tapestry in shades of green. From the bridge, I watched hundreds of ducks paddling on Rost Lake and admired a picturesque farmstead overlooking water and forest. Gazing upon this setting, I could understand why early settlers chose to make this place home.

All too soon, it was time to head back to the trailhead. After hiking 1 mile, Sandy and I made a short side trip to School Section Lake. I enjoyed getting a closer look at this scenic lake, then retraced my steps to the trailhead.

SANDY'S NOTES ON THE HIKE

I love all the smells of the woods and wanted to sniff everywhere I went in the aspen forest. Fortunately, Susan wanted to linger on this hike as well, so she didn't mind my taking time to explore the trail.

WHAT'S FOR LUNCH?

The bridge between Eramosh and Rost lakes is a perfect picnic spot, but Bob joined Sandy and me for lunch in the shady picnic area near Lake Metigoshe State Park swimming beach. I always enjoy a swim after a hike on a hot day and there's a modern lavatory here. We grilled brats and served them up with pickles, condiments, buns, fresh tomatoes, chips and cold drinks. Convenience stores and restaurants are located outside the park boundaries, but some are open only during summer months.

ANOTHER FAVORITE HIKE

LAKE METIGOSHE STATE PARK
OLD OAK TRAIL (1.5 MILES)

If you enjoy hiking next to lakes, this loop trail is for you. The hike starts and finishes at the same location and features the most scenic section of Old Oak Trail.

The well-marked trailhead is 0.5 mile north of the park entrance station, where you should stop and pick up an interpretive brochure. You'll find a vault toilet across the road from the trailhead. Leashed dogs are allowed.

The first section of the trail offers nice views of School Section Lake, but my favorite part of the hike is on the peninsula that juts into the middle of the lake. Sometimes you walk along the middle of the peninsula and at other times you hike right along the shoreline. A bridge connects the peninsula to an island, but on my most recent trip the bridge was in disrepair. When the bridge is repaired, an interesting part of the hike will be restored.

At the southeast end of the peninsula, leave Old Oak Trail and take the path leading up to a campground. Enter the campground, turn right and follow the campground road a short distance until you see a wide path leading to the right. Follow this path until you rejoin Old Oak Trail and retrace your steps back to the trailhead.

QUESTIONS?

Lake Metigoshe State Park, 701.263.4651, www.parkrec.nd.gov/parks/lmsp.htm

BUTTE SAINT PAUL HISTORIC SITE

HIKE TO BUTTE SAINT PAUL

What makes this hike spectacular? **Butte Saint Paul is the highest point on the southern edge of the Turtle Mountains. The brief walk to the top rewards hikers with a panoramic, southern view of the countryside below. Chippewa Indians call this overlook Place Where One Can See Forever.**

AT A GLANCE

HIKE TO BUTTE SAINT PAUL

Map:	**Page 40**
Location:	**Butte Saint Paul Historic Site**
Nearest town:	**Bottineau**
Length:	**0.5-mile loop**
Elevation change:	**120 feet**
Dogs:	**Allowed on leashes**
Fees:	**None**
Services at trailhead:	**Information sign**

DIRECTIONS TO TRAILHEAD

From Bottineau, go 12 miles east on Highway 5 until you reach the Butte Saint Paul Historic Site sign. Turn left and proceed north 4 miles on a gravel road until you see another sign indicating an east turn. Follow the narrow lane approximately 0.5 mile to the parking area. The trailhead is on the north side, adjacent to the information sign.

SUSAN'S NOTES ON THE HIKE

Butte Saint Paul was named by Father George Belcourt. A Catholic missionary in the middle 1800s, Father Belcourt was a great friend of the Indian people and often walked long distances to do his work. The town of Belcourt, east on Highway 5, is named for him.

In January 1850, Father Belcourt set out on a journey. The weather had been pleasant, but a sudden blizzard forced him to find protection among the trees below a large hill in the Turtle Mountains. Thankful for surviving the blizzard, Father Belcourt erected a cross on top of the hill and named it Butte Saint Paul.

The trail climbs sharply uphill to a prairie area. In August, Bob and I found purple blazing star (liatris), goldenrod and purple asters blooming here. Within 0.25 mile you will reach a stone cairn erected in 1933 by Dunseith-area citizens to mark the historic site.

The Turtle Mountains may not qualify as mountains in other states, but in North Dakota the 600-to-800-foot elevation gain from the prairie floor to the top of the hills is impressive. We took our time absorbing the fantastic view from our 700-foot vantage point, estimating we could see as far as 30 to 40 miles to the south.

The loop trail continues downhill, offering a few more fine views of the area. Soon bur oak, green ash and chokecherry trees obscure the horizon, and you return to the parking lot only with memories of those panoramic, prairie views.

WHAT'S FOR LUNCH?

Since this is a short hike, we packed only fruit-and-nut trail mix and snacked at the top of Butte Saint Paul. Bottineau, 16 miles southwest, has a number of restaurants and a grocery store for buying picnic supplies.

SANDY'S NOTES ON THE HIKE

After riding in the car for three hours, I was ready for a longer outing, but this short hike up the hill – recommended to Susan by a friend – was fine. We all enjoyed exploring this historic site.

QUESTIONS?

Lake Metigoshe State Park, 701.263.4651,
www.parkrec.nd.gov/parks/lmsp.htm

INTERNATIONAL PEACE GARDEN
FORMAL GARDENS BORDER WALK

What makes this hike spectacular? The International Peace Garden, established on the U.S.-Canada border in 1932, celebrates world peace and the world's longest unfortified border. The Formal Gardens Border Walk takes you back and forth across the border, through colorful annual and perennial flower beds. Even when the gardens aren't in bloom, the formal landscaping, terraces, peace tower, peace chapel, interpretive center and conservatory make this a wonderful walk.

AT A GLANCE

FORMAL GARDENS BORDER WALK

Map:	Page 41
Trail location:	International Peace Garden
Nearest town:	Dunseith
Length:	2 mile loop
Change in elevation:	Less than 50 feet
Dogs:	Allowed on leashes
Fees:	Park entrance fee
Services at trailhead:	Souvenir shop with lavatory
Special note:	International customs regulations apply

DIRECTIONS TO TRAILHEAD

The International Peace Garden is 13 miles north of Dunseith on Highway 3. Turn right after you enter the park. To your immediate left is a large parking lot. The hike starts at the gift shop at the west end of this parking lot. There is no marked trailhead.

SUSAN'S NOTES ON THE HIKE

Bob, Sandy and I enjoyed this hike in late August when all of the annual flowers were in full bloom. The hike starts in the formal area of the garden, next to the gift shop. Here you'll find terraces, fountains and flowerbeds. Take time to explore and take lots of pictures. It's not surprising many weddings take place here.

When you are ready to see more, take the walkway on the Canadian side (to your right) to the sunken garden. This area features perennial flowers. It's surrounded by a large, gated fence to keep out moose and deer.

Proceeding along the walkway you may hear the carillon in the bell tower, you'll pass beneath the magnificent Peace Tower and you can visit Peace Chapel. It's been almost 200 years since the Convention of 1818 established the 49th Parallel as the boundary between the United States and Canada. As I stroll along, I always reflect on how lucky I am to live within 200 miles of an unarmed, international border. So many people around the world are not so fortunate.

You'll loop back on the U.S. side of walkway, which will take you past the 9/11 Memorial. Made from 10 steel girders taken from the former World Trade Center, the memorial honors those killed in the Sept. 11, 2001, terrorist attack.

Be sure to stop in the impressive Interpretive Center and Conservatory, where you'll find a café and gift shop. Proceed east on the U.S. side of the gardens to the floral clock near the entrance area. Planted each spring, the clock is a special feature of the park.

Every time I visit the Peace Garden, I am thankful for the Canadian and American citizens who have spent more than 75 years developing this 2,339-acre park. It's impressive to know the park is owned by a non-profit corporation and that funding for the structures and gardens comes from private, non-profit organizations in both countries.

SANDY'S NOTES ON THE HIKE

I enjoyed meeting some new people at the International Peace Garden. Susan wouldn't let me drink from the ponds or fountains, so I was glad I carried my own water in my dog backpack. When Susan entered Peace Chapel, I stayed outside with Bob. There are some places a dog just doesn't enter.

ANOTHER FAVORITE HIKE

INTERNATIONAL PEACE GARDEN
LAKEVIEW HIKING TRAIL (1.25 MILES)

Lakeview Hiking Trail or Rum Runners' Trail is the oldest trail in the International Peace Garden. In fact, the trail pre-dates the garden's founding by 12 years. This grassy, loop trail takes you into the quaking aspen forest and to the shores of four Canadian lakes.

As you drive the loop road on the Canadian side of the Peace Garden, you will see a sign that says Nature Trail and a parking lot. The trailhead for Lakeview Hiking Trail is located here. Leashed dogs are allowed.

On a hot August day, the quaking aspen forest provides welcome shade. After hiking about 0.25 mile, Lakeview Hiking Trail comes to a junction with another hiking trail, which is not indicated on the International Peace Garden Map. Bob, Sandy and I followed the path for about 0.12 mile and were treated to views of two more lakes. We then retraced our steps back to Lakeview Trail.

Continuing on the loop trail, we saw two lakes with beaver lodges and hiked past boulders and rocks left behind thousands of years ago by receding glaciers.

WHAT'S FOR LUNCH?

We purchased lunch at Border Walk Café in the Interpretive Center and Conservatory. This beautiful facility is open year round. For a picnic, I recommend Maple Picnic Area, a shady spot on the edge of Lake Stormon in the Canadian side of the park.

QUESTIONS?

～ The International Peace Garden, 888.432.6733, www.peacegarden.com

TURTLE MOUNTAIN STATE FOREST

BLACK LAKE TRAIL IN STRAWBERRY LAKE RECREATION AREA

What makes this hike spectacular? On this shady hike you'll explore Turtle Mountain State Forest, North Dakota's largest state forest. Black Lake Trail follows the shore of Strawberry Lake, passes through bur oak forest and small meadows to Black Lake, traversing small hills and ravines on the southwest slope of the Turtle Mountains. Be sure to combine this hike with a visit to Mystical Horizons, North Dakota's Stonehenge for the 21st Century, 1 mile west on Highway 43.

DIRECTIONS TO TRAILHEAD

Strawberry Lake Recreation Area is in Turtle Mountain State Forest, 11 miles northwest of Bottineau on Highway 43. Park in the parking lot adjacent to the Strawberry Lake boat ramp. You'll find the trailhead just to the right of the fishing dock.

AT A GLANCE

BLACK LAKE TRAIL IN STRAWBERRY LAKE RECREATION AREA

Map:	Page 42
Trail location:	Turtle Mountain State Forest
Nearest town:	Bottineau
Length:	3 miles round trip
Change in elevation:	60 feet
Dogs:	Allowed on leashes
Fees:	None
Services at trailhead:	None
Hunting alert:	Avoid hiking here during hunting seasons

SUSAN'S NOTES ON THE HIKE

Less than 2 percent of the land in North Dakota is forested – the smallest area of any state in the country – so forestland is a precious resource. With more than 20 miles of hiking trails, 7,000-acre Turtle Mountain State Forest provides many opportunities to enjoy this rare North Dakota ecosystem.

Bob, Sandy and I hiked this portion of the Black Lake Trail in mid August. The hike begins in the mixed bur oak, quaking aspen and green ash forest along the shores of Strawberry Lake. The trail occasionally curves inland to skirt marshy areas.

At the south end of Strawberry Lake the trail widens to a wide grassy path through a mature bur oak forest. After 0.5 mile, you will arrive at a junction with a trail on your right that leads to the west; do not take this trail. Continue south on Black Lake Trail up and down some small hills and across two small, wood bridges. After hiking for about 0.5 mile, you'll see some open meadows.

The way to Black Lake is marked with a sign. The trail leads through woods adjacent to open meadows. In August, the wild asters and goldenrod were in bloom. With its mix of wide meadow views, forest shade and woodlands sounds, I loved walking through this area.

We didn't stay long at Black Lake. A small body of water with a reedy shore, it had more bugs than on any other part of our hike and we quickly departed. Turns out we liked the trail much more than the destination and enjoyed our favorite spots one more time as we retraced our way to the trailhead.

SANDY'S NOTES ON THE HIKE

I loved swimming next to the boat ramp in Strawberry Lake. Although moose live in the state forest, we didn't see any. We did, however, see and hear numerous birds along the trail.

WHAT'S FOR LUNCH?

After a quick dip in a chilly Strawberry Lake, we ate our picnic lunch at a picnic table adjacent to the swimming beach. We brought our ingredients in our cooler and when we were ready to eat we filled pita pocket bread with a mixture of vacuum-packed tuna, diced apples, celery and a little mayonnaise. Our lunch also included ginger cookies, green grapes and beverages. Vault toilets are located in this part of Strawberry Lake Recreation Area.

QUESTIONS?

~ North Dakota Forest Service, 701.228.3700, www.ndsu.edu/ndfs/state_forests/

~ Mystical Horizons, www.turtlemountains.org

Across the meadow a small backcountry pond sparkled in the sunshine.

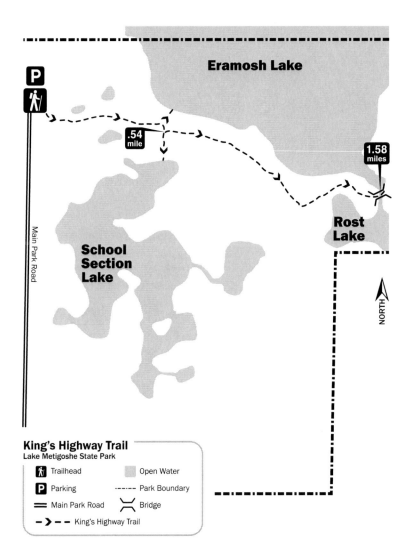

King's Highway Trail
Lake Metigoshe State Park

🚶 Trailhead		Open Water
P Parking	-----	Park Boundary
Main Park Road	Bridge
- > - - King's Highway Trail		

Want to know more about this trail?
TURN TO PAGE 27

We took our time absorbing the fantastic view from our 700-foot vantage point, estimating we could see as far as 30 to 40 miles to the south.

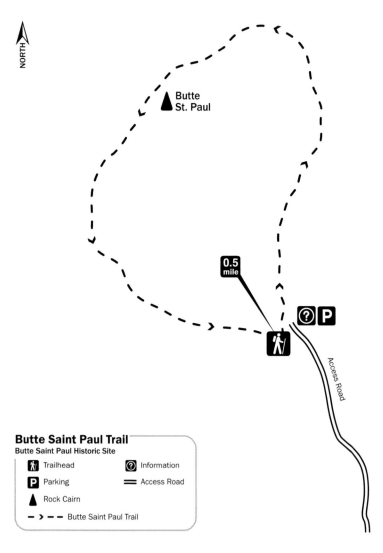

Butte Saint Paul Trail
Butte Saint Paul Historic Site

- Trailhead
- Parking
- Rock Cairn
- – > – – Butte Saint Paul Trail
- Information
- Access Road

Want to know more about this trail?
TURN TO PAGE 31

The hike starts in the formal area of the garden, next to the gift shop. Here you'll find terraces, fountains and flowerbeds.

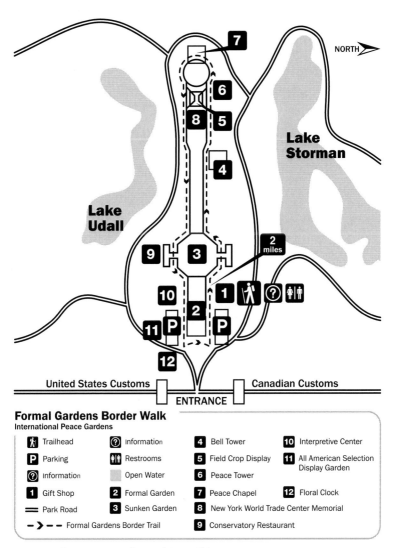

NORTH

Lake Storman

Lake Udall

2 miles

United States Customs

Canadian Customs

ENTRANCE

Formal Gardens Border Walk
International Peace Gardens

🥾 Trailhead	ⓘ Information	**4** Bell Tower	**10** Interpretive Center
P Parking	🚻 Restrooms	**5** Field Crop Display	**11** All American Selection Display Garden
ⓘ Information	Open Water	**6** Peace Tower	
1 Gift Shop	**2** Formal Garden	**7** Peace Chapel	**12** Floral Clock
━━ Park Road	**3** Sunken Garden	**8** New York World Trade Center Memorial	
➤ Formal Gardens Border Trail		**9** Conservatory Restaurant	

Want to know more about this trail?
TURN TO PAGE 33

At the south end of Strawberry Lake the trail widens to a wide grassy path through a mature bur oak forest

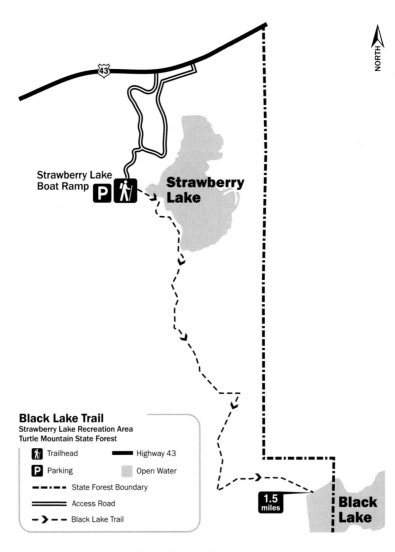

Want to know more about this trail?
TURN TO PAGE 36

MY NOTES

I stop to examine
A patch of native prairie and
Find an intricate tapestry of
Grasses and forbs.
                    — *Susan Wefald*

AREA ATTRACTIONS

Sheyenne River Valley National Scenic Byway, a beautiful drive at any time of the year, follows the Sheyenne River for 63 miles from Valley City to Lisbon. Interpretive signs along the route point out interesting features.

~ Fort Ransom State Historic Site, just west of the town of Fort Ransom, marks the location of a military post established in 1867.

~ Fort Ransom State Park offers camping, hiking trails, horseback riding, kayaking, canoe rentals and transport services.

WHERE TO HIKE

● *Fort Ransom State Park, Fort Ransom*

● *Sheyenne State Forest/North Country National Scenic Trail, Fort Ransom*

● *Sheyenne National Grassland/North Country National Scenic Trail, South of Casselton*

~ Maple Creek Crossing State Historic Site, an important landmark in the early settlement of Dakota Territory, is 8 miles northwest of Leonard.

AREA ACCOMMODATIONS

~ Fort Ransom State Park has a nice campground.

~ Fort Ransom, Valley City and Casselton offer several options for accommodations.

~ A horse camp and RV park is adjacent to the Sheyenne National Grassland, about 25 miles south of Casselton.

FORT RANSOM STATE PARK
VALLEY VIEW TRAIL

What makes this hike spectacular? The Sheyenne River Valley has a quiet beauty. The grasslands along the valley, amid the tall bur oaks, are described by locals as meadows rather than prairie. The rolling hills have gentle slopes. The hike features beautiful views of the Sheyenne River Valley. After a 0.75-mile hike down the grass-and-tree-covered slope to the valley, you'll arrive at Sunne Farm. Here you can sit on the front steps of a log cabin built in 1875 and view other farm buildings added during the 75 years the Sunne family farmed here.

AT A GLANCE
VALLEY VIEW TRAIL

Map:	Page 56
Location:	Fort Ransom State Park
Nearest town:	Fort Ransom
Length:	1.5 miles round trip
Elevation change:	160 feet
Dogs:	Allowed on leashes
Fees:	Park entrance fee
Services at trailhead:	Interpretive signs

DIRECTIONS TO TRAILHEAD

Fort Ransom State Park is on the Sheyenne River Valley National Scenic Byway, 2 miles north of the town of Fort Ransom. The trailhead is about 1.5 miles from the park visitor center. Follow the signs to the scenic overlook, where you'll find parking and the trailhead marker.

SUSAN'S NOTES ON THE HIKE

Spring was definitely in the air in late May when Sandy and I visited Fort Ransom State Park. The river valley was lush green, accented by the purples of blooming lilac hedgerows and pink and white of flowering apple trees.

This hike begins at a scenic overlook with long views of the river valley. As I walked downhill I was so captivated by the distant scenery I almost missed seeing clusters of sumac growing on the hillside. I didn't know sumac grew here, but later learned it's common in the area. Chokecherry trees were in bloom near the trail and I could smell their strong, sweet aroma from quite a distance.

Although you can drive to the Sunne farm site, I loved arriving on foot. I sat down on the front step of the homesteaders' original cabin and thought about what life might have been like for the Norwegian family who settled in this lovely spot. They built the cabin in 1875 and in 1914 erected a mail-order barn, its parts numbered to aid assembly. The large, red barn still stands along with other buildings added to the property over its years of operation.

I found this beautiful spot filled with spirits of the past and – as I walked back up the hill –I thought of the many Sunne family members who had probably taken this same walk over the years.

WHAT'S FOR LUNCH?

A farmhouse serves as the state park office and visitor center and the shady front yard is a perfect spot for picnicking, but I opted to dine in nearby Fort Ransom. Located about 2 miles south of the park, Fort Ransom is small – only about 100 residents – but the community offers great hospitality for individual travelers and draws many visitors with festivals and special events.

SANDY'S NOTES ON THE HIKE

While Susan sat on a bench enjoying the view from the parking lot's scenic overlook, I found a stick on which to chew and lay there while we both watched the sunset. After a lot of hiking, I was ready to relax.

ANOTHER FAVORITE HIKE

FORT RANSOM STATE PARK
LITTLE TWIG NATURE TRAIL (0.75 MILE)

If you're up for more hiking in Fort Ransom State Park I recommend Little Twig Nature Trail. I love trails with bridges and this one has four that crisscross a creek. If you pick up a brochure at the visitor center you can turn this into a self-guided nature hike.

The 0.75-mile loop trail starts at Abel's Hole picnic shelter, about 0.5 mile from the park visitor center. Leashed dogs are allowed.

In late May, the swollen creek was a true babbling brook, a rare find in North Dakota. The sound of water tumbling over rocks and boulders is so refreshing. I saw ducks swimming in the deeper pools and yellow marsh marigolds blooming in the creek bed. The level trail follows the creek for about 0.5 miles before it loops back across open meadows.

QUESTIONS?

Fort Ransom State Park, 701.973.4331,
www.parkrec.nd.gov/parks/frsp.htm

SHEYENNE STATE FOREST
MINERAL SPRINGS AND WATERFALL TRAIL

What makes this hike spectacular? **This hike takes you from the wooded floor of the Sheyenne River Valley to the top of native prairie bluffs overlooking the valley. The trail provides grand views up and down the Sheyenne River Valley and leads to North Dakota's only natural waterfall.**

AT A GLANCE
MINERAL SPRINGS AND WATERFALL TRAIL

Map:	**Page 57**
Location:	**Sheyenne State Forest**
Nearest town:	**Fort Ransom**
Length:	**4 miles round trip**
Elevation change:	**165 feet**
Dogs:	**Allowed on leashes**
Fees:	**None**
Services at trailhead:	**Interpretive signs and trail map**
Hunting alert:	**Avoid hiking here during hunting seasons**

DIRECTIONS TO TRAILHEAD

This trail begins in Sheyenne State Forest, 3 miles southeast of Fort Ransom on the Sheyenne River Valley National Scenic Byway. Turn south at the Sheyenne State Forest sign and cross historic Martinson Bridge. You'll see the trailhead and interpretive signs next to the parking area.

SUSAN'S NOTES ON THE HIKE

The waterfall on this hike is small, but I love all waterfalls and there's much to see along the way. The Mineral Springs and Waterfall Trail are part of the North Country National Scenic Trail. A work in progress, when completed this national trail will link scenic, natural, historic and cultural areas in seven states and will become the longest continuous hiking trail in the United States.

Sandy and I took this hike in mid July. The trail begins on the dirt road adjacent to an old farm; watch for the signed entrance to North Country National Scenic Hiking Trail. The dirt trail branches to the right and is clearly marked with blue markers and blue paint on the trees.

Mineral Springs Trail proceeds up and down the wooded hillsides for 1.6 miles to Mineral Spring. At the top of the hills are prairie meadows. These areas offer great views of the Sheyenne River Valley, which was formed about 13,000 years ago by meltwater from the Wisconsin glacier. The receding glacier left behind many large and small granite boulders.

I enjoyed hiking through the forest areas, but I loved coming up out of the forest and experiencing the open spaces of the prairie meadows. Non-native plants dominate some of these meadows, while others are filled with native mixed-grass prairie wildflowers.

In one spot along the trail, I looked up and saw pale purple coneflowers on the hill above me. I climbed up to take a closer look and not only found coneflowers, but also leadplant, bluebells, western salsify, wooly verbena, yellow upright prairie coneflowers and others I couldn't identify. Sandy and I sat in their midst, enjoying the view and the smell of the land.

As you near Mineral Spring you cross a wood bridge over a small creek in a rather muddy area. A short distance from the bridge the creek bed widens into a small, side valley of the Sheyenne River. At the place where Mineral Spring flows into the creek you'll find a picnic table in a grassy area shaded by mature basswood trees. I stopped for a few minutes to enjoy the peaceful sounds of birds singing and treetops ruffling in the wind.

Before reaching the waterfall you'll pass meadowlands and stands of bur oak, American basswood and green ash growing near a small creek. You'll also cross two more bridges; after the first bridge a sign will direct you to the left and inform you the waterfall is 400 feet ahead.

The woodsy glen adjacent to the falls is equipped with a picnic table and fire grate. While Sandy explored the creek and took a drink, I sat and enjoyed the sound of the running water and the beauty of the day.

I took my time on my return trip, stopping to listen, breathing deeply, enjoying even grander views of the river valley and looking more closely at wildflowers, trees, fungi and other flora and fauna along the way.

SANDY'S NOTES ON THE HIKE

Since it was a cool day, and because water is accessible in two places along the hike, I didn't carry water in my dog backpack. I took long drinks at the bridge crossing the creek at Mineral Springs and near the waterfall. I loved rolling in the grass near the Mineral Springs picnic table while Susan took a short rest.

WHAT'S FOR LUNCH?

Next time I hike this trail I'll bring along my husband, Bob, and we'll picnic at the waterfall. I'll pack some steaks for grilling, German potato salad, carrot sticks and bread wrapped in foil for easy heating. Although Sandy and I saw wood piled near the grill, just in case I'll bring along some charcoal. If you don't have picnic supplies, you can find lunch in the town of Fort Ransom.

ANOTHER FAVORITE HIKE

SHEYENNE STATE FOREST
OAK RIDGE HIKING TRAIL (1.25 MILES)

This forest trail winds up and down an oak ridge on slopes above the Sheyenne River Valley. You'll explore a narrow, forested ravine and visit good viewpoints of the surrounding countryside. Oak Ridge Hiking Trail is part of North Country National Scenic Trail.

The loop trail starts 0.5 mile south of Martinson Bridge, adjacent to a small parking area. Leashed dogs are allowed. Hunting is allowed in this area, so this trail should be avoided during hunting seasons.

The trail follows a wooded hillside. After about 0.25 miles, take the right fork to the top of a sumac-covered ridge overlooking the Sheyenne River Valley. You'll hike down a forested ravine, climb up and down an oak ridge and soon be back at the trailhead.

QUESTIONS?

~ North Dakota Forest Service, 701.228.3700, www.ndsu.edu/ndfs/state_forests/

SHEYENNE NATIONAL GRASSLAND
HIKE TO IRON SPRINGS

What makes this hike spectacular? On the hike to Iron Springs, a section of North Country National Scenic Trail, you'll explore an oak savannah, a rare ecosystem in North Dakota where groves of old bur oak trees are interspersed with rolling prairie on sand hills. Named for a spring-fed prairie stream, this backcountry trail has only a few fences to remind you that you're not crossing the prairie as a pioneer.

AT A GLANCE

HIKE TO IRON SPRINGS

Map:	**Page 58**
Location:	**Sheyenne National Grassland**
Nearest town:	**Casselton**
Length:	**8 miles roundtrip**
Elevation change:	**Less than 50 feet**
Dogs:	**Allowed without leashes but under control**
Fees:	**None**
Services at trailhead:	**Sign with trail map**
Hunting alert:	**Avoid hiking here during hunting seasons**

DIRECTIONS TO TRAILHEAD

The trailhead is in the northeast section of Sheyenne National Grassland, 25 miles south of Casselton. Take Highway 18 south of Casselton to 1 mile south of Leonard. Then travel 2 miles south and then 0.5 mile east on dirt roads to County Road 23. Cross the Sheyenne River on County Road 23. After passing Zion Church and a horse camp/RV park, watch for signs for Sheyenne National Grassland Trailhead.

SUSAN'S NOTES ON THE HIKE

Sheyenne National Grassland encompasses more than 70,000 acres of grassland in southeastern North Dakota. It's one of the few places in the state where tallgrass prairie still exists. The distinctive landscape features hills created from sand deposited thousands of years ago by the Sheyenne River as it carried glacial meltwater eastward into Lake Agassiz, an ancient lake that once covered much of the Red River Valley. The sand deposits blew into sand dunes and formed the sand hills we see today along the Sheyenne River.

The hike to Iron Springs is part of a 28-mile section of the North Country Scenic Trail that passes through Sheyenne National

Grassland. Sandy and I hiked this trail in mid July. The gravel trail is well marked and easy to follow. Leashing your dog isn't required, but a leash will help you keep your dog under control should you encounter cattle, horseback riders, bicyclists or other hikers.

The trail starts in a cow pasture. There were quite a few cows present when Sandy and I arrived. Since I didn't know how the cows would react to my dog, I drove my car about a third of a mile south of the parking lot and we started our hike where the trail crosses the road and heads west. We didn't see any other cattle on the hike.

The first part of the trail goes through a marsh and I had to abandon the trail often because it was covered with several inches of water. Adjacent marsh grass kept me out of the mud and water and soon we were hiking again on dry land. Of course Sandy had a great time splashing his way along the trail.

The trail has five gates that must be lifted to open and lowered to close. The gates are easy to manage and allow hikers and cattle to co-exist. When correctly managed, cattle grazing is good for native prairie areas. The fences and gates allow ranchers to rotate the cattle to prevent overgrazing.

I love hiking through oak savannah, with its alternating stands of bur oak and mixed-grass prairie meadows. Among the protected plants that grow here is the rare western prairie white fringed orchid. I didn't see any along the trail, but I did find a few blooming in other parts of the grassland. Unfortunately, I did see huge patches of leafy spurge growing along the trail. This noxious weed thrives in sandy soil. Although national grassland staff members try to control it with beetles, goats and chemicals, the leafy spurge keeps spreading.

When you've hiked a little over 2 miles and gone through the fourth gate you will see a windmill and a small pond. Continuing west, you will note small changes in the landscape. Beyond the fifth gate, you'll see more grassland and fewer bur oak groves, more eastern cottonwood trees in low spots and more lead plant and sage. When you see four tall eastern cottonwoods near a bridge you'll know Iron Springs is just ahead.

Iron Springs has eroded a small gully into the prairie. Sandy and I crossed the bridge and climbed down the grassy slope to wade in the cool water. It was blissful resting there, smelling the sweet grass, watching dragonflies swoop above the water and feeling the sun's warmth on my skin. In this moment I felt like one of the prairie women depicted in the paintings of famed South Dakota artist Harvey Dunn.

The return trip was equally satisfying and seemed shorter than the hike west.

SANDY'S NOTES ON THE HIKE

I wore my dog backpack so I could carry my own water. Susan removed my pack when we arrived at the stream. I had a great time playing in the water and chasing dragonflies. We saw one white-tailed deer on the trail and heard songbirds in the oak groves.

WHAT'S FOR LUNCH?

The trail turnaround point is a perfect spot for lunch, but since Sandy and I had traveled by car for several hours we ate our lunch before we started hiking. I brought along a container of wild rice salad made with cold chicken, cooked wild rice, chopped celery, dried cranberries, walnuts and raspberry salad dressing. My meal also included a muffin, fresh plums and a beverage. If you want to purchase food, several restaurants and grocery stores can be found 25 miles north of the trailhead in Casselton.

QUESTIONS?

Dakota Prairie Grasslands, 701.683.4342, www.fs.fed.us/r1/dakotaprairie

As I walked downhill I was so captivated by the distant scenery I almost missed seeing clusters of sumac growing on the hillside.

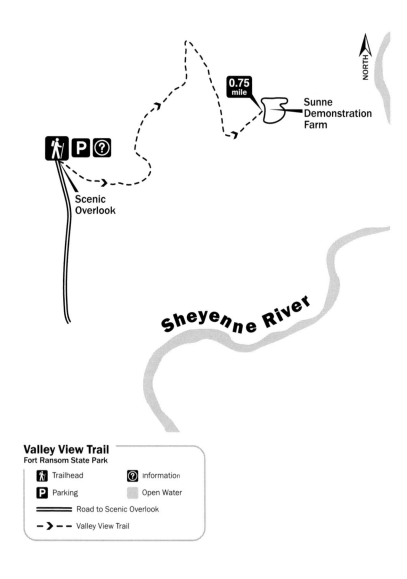

Want to know more about this trail?

TURN TO PAGE 46

A short distance from the bridge the creek bed widens into a small side valley of the Sheyenne River.

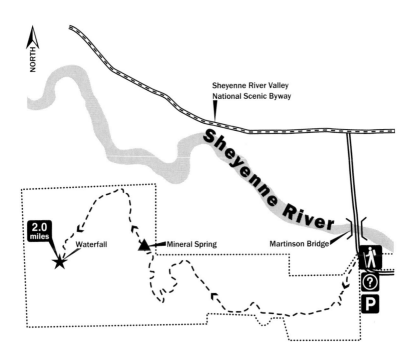

Mineral Spring & Waterfall Trail
Sheyenne State Forest

🚶 Trailhead	★ Waterfall		
P Parking	▲ Mineral Spring		
ⓘ Information	······· State Forest Boundary		
Open Water	═══ Access Road		
▄▄▄ Sheyenne River Valley National Scenic Byway			
➤ Mineral Spring & Waterfall Trail			

Want to know more about this trail?
TURN TO PAGE 49

I love hiking through oak savannah, with its alternating stands of bur oak and mixed grass prairie meadows.

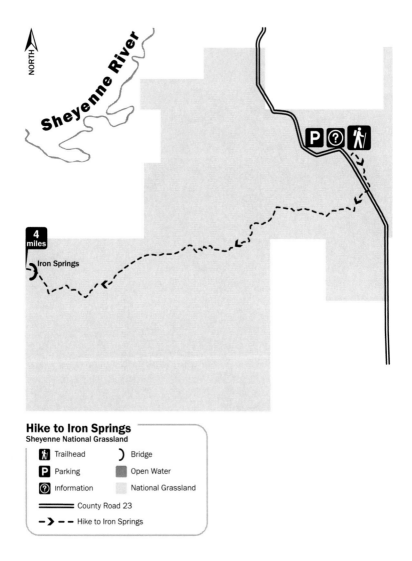

Hike to Iron Springs
Sheyenne National Grassland

🚶 Trailhead	)	Bridge
🅿 Parking		Open Water
ⓘ Information		National Grassland
═══ County Road 23		
–>– – Hike to Iron Springs		

Want to know more about this trail?
TURN TO PAGE 52

MY NOTES

FOUR

LITTLE MISSOURI RIVER BADLANDS

Scanning the grand horizon
From the top of a badlands butte
I feel
Free as a bird.

— Susan Wefald

AREA ATTRACTIONS

Medora is a tourist hub, with a professional outdoor variety show performed nightly in June, July and August. Medora also is home to Theodore Roosevelt National Park Visitor Center, featuring Roosevelt's ranching cabin and numerous exhibits about his ranching activities. Other attractions include the North Dakota Cowboy Hall of Fame and Chateau de Mores Historic Site.

~ Drive through Theodore Roosevelt National Park South Unit to see beautiful badlands vistas and experience a North American safari seeing prairie dogs, bison, wild horses, pronghorns and other native species.

~ Killdeer Mountains Four Bears Scenic Byway follows Highway 22 from Manning to New Town and passes by Little Missouri State Park. Among historic sites in the area is the scene of the Battle of the Killdeer Mountains.

WHERE TO HIKE

- *Theodore Roosevelt National Park, South Unit, Medora*
- *Theodore Roosevelt National Park, North Unit, Watford City*
- *Little Missouri State Park, Killdeer*
- *Little Missouri National Grassland, Watford City*
- *Maah Daah Hey Trail, Grassy Butte*

~ Guided trail rides of Little Missouri State Park and horse rentals are available near the park entrance.

~ Drive through Theodore Roosevelt National Park's North Unit to observe stunning badlands scenery and herds of bison grazing along the Little Missouri River.

~ Watford City, 19 miles north of Theodore Roosevelt National Park's North Unit, has a municipal water park, a large western-themed children's playground and a golf course. Long X Trading Post on Main Street includes a pioneer museum, visitor information and the largest petrified tree stump ever found in North Dakota. The 60-million-year-old stump, is 6 feet in diameter and 7 feet tall.

~ Old Grassy Butte Post Office Historic Site was built in 1912 of logs and sod. Now it's a nationally registered historic site and free admission museum in Grassy Butte.

AREA ACCOMMODATIONS

~ Theodore Roosevelt National Park's South Unit offers a large shady campground near the Little Missouri River. The North Unit has a large, shady campground near the Little Missouri River.

~ The cities of Medora and Dickinson, in the south, and Watford City, in the north, provide many options for lodging; ranchers in this area also offer cabins for rent.

THEODORE ROOSEVELT NATIONAL PARK – SOUTH UNIT

PAINTED CANYON TRAIL

What makes this hike spectacular? **Theodore Roosevelt National Park is filled with tremendous views of the North Dakota badlands and the Painted Canyon Visitor Center overlooks one of the most scenic areas of the park. This trail allows the hiker to explore the floor of the Painted Canyon with its distinctive geologic formations, including petrified wood stumps, bentonite clay benches and small, rock-capped, sandstone pillars called hoodoos. Native prairie grasslands and Rocky Mountain Juniper trees enhance the rugged beauty.**

AT A GLANCE
PAINTED CANYON TRAIL

Map:	**Page 85**
Location:	**Painted Canyon Visitor Center**
Nearest Town:	**Medora**
Length:	**4 miles round trip**
Elevation change:	**285 feet**
Dogs:	**No dogs allowed on trails**
Fees:	**None at Painted Canyon Visitor Center**
Services at trailhead:	**Painted Canyon Visitor Center and trail are open mid-April to early November; call ahead for specific dates. The Medora visitor center and other national park trails are open year round.**
Special note:	**Trail hazardous when wet**

DIRECTIONS TO TRAILHEAD

Painted Canyon Visitor Center is 7 miles east of Medora on I-94/ Exit 32. The trailhead is at the east end of the parking lot or to your right as you face the canyon. Look for a dirt service road leading past weather station equipment and follow it east. There is no trailhead marker. The entire route is marked by slender, metal poles driven into the ground.

SUSAN'S NOTES ON THE HIKE

This national park is named for President Theodore Roosevelt, who ranched in this area in the 1880s. T.R. loved the North Dakota badlands and wrote extensively about his experiences here, which helped shape his thoughts on nature conservation.

Painted Canyon Trail follows the rim of the canyon about 0.5 mile and then descends into the canyon. A short way into the descent there's a hikers' register for sharing thoughts and reporting home states. It's fun reading other hikers' comments, but from this vantage point on a rather steep section of trail, it's even more enjoyable spotting unusual badlands formations.

As you travel across the North Dakota prairie the land doesn't give away many of its past secrets, but in the badlands these secrets are revealed. For more than 500,000 years, weather and water in the Little Missouri River floodplain have eroded the land into ridges, knobs and conical hills, revealing layers of sediment deposited as many as 60 million years ago. Some layers contain clay created from volcanic ash. In the sandstone layers you may find large, fossilized tree stumps.

My friend Gail and I hiked here in early November. Although the prairie grasses were dormant and caramel colored, we enjoyed observing the various shapes and sizes of grass and wildflower seedpods. This part of the trail goes up and down through many small ravines among Rocky Mountain juniper trees. While the ravines were dry in early November, they can carry great amounts of water during spring snow melt and after summer thunderstorms.

We were alert for bison – commonly known as buffalo – and while we didn't see any on this hike, we did spy many, fresh buffalo pies.

Soon we stopped to look at four large pieces of petrified wood. Here's how petrified wood is made: Picture a large forest of trees near a river. The river overflows and sediment covers the base of the trees. The trees die and eventually rot away, but the tree stumps are preserved in the sediment. Millions of years pass and the stumps turn to stone as minerals in the sediment take the place of the wood cells. Variations in color come from the minerals that permeate the wood. That's why the petrified wood in the Southwest tends to be more colorful than the petrified wood in Theodore Roosevelt National Park.

Although there are large pieces of petrified wood along the trail, originally all were embedded in a layer of sandstone, deposited approximately 50 million years ago. Continuing along the trail, we soon saw a large eroded cliff that revealed many different layers of sediment. About half way up the cliff, many large pieces of petrified wood were sticking out of a layer of sandstone. Also, near the bottom of this cliff are pillars of sandstone topped with harder rock called a cap rock. These are called hoodoos.

After hiking up and down through a dry creek bed, the trail crosses a bentonite clay bench, a flat terrace of land on a slope above the streambed. Bentonite clay was formed from volcanic ash deposited millions of years ago. At this spot in the badlands it is dark blue-gray and when dry it has a popcorn appearance. You do not want to walk on it when it is wet. It is extremely greasy and slippery. I know this from personal experience.

Soon the trail leads you through less rugged prairie grasslands. To the west is an exposed, cutbank of red clinker. Known locally as scoria, red clinker is clay that has been baked by a buried, burning coal vein. These layers of red rock give the Painted Canyon its colorful appearance. Along the trail, look for large chunks of dark red rock, covered with grey green lichen. These also are chunks of clinker.

A wood post marks the end of Painted Canyon Trail and the intersection with Upper Paddock Creek Trail. Before we turned around and hiked back to the visitor center, we sat down for a rest and a snack. A golden eagle made a turn in the sky and came to take a look at us. The sun was warm on our backs and we took off our jackets. The sagebrush around us turned our thoughts to eating turkey dressing soon. Fall can be a great time for a hike in the badlands.

SANDY'S NOTES ON THE HIKE

Dogs are not allowed on national park trails so Susan left me at home.

WHAT'S FOR LUNCH?

Gail and I brought along a picnic lunch, which we ate in one of the shelters near the visitor center overlooking the badlands. In addition to our ham-on-rye sandwiches, we had sweet pickles, potato chips, apples and popcorn balls. Medora, 7 miles west, is the closest town to pick up picnic supplies or purchase lunch.

ANOTHER FAVORITE HIKE

PAINTED CANYON NATURE TRAIL (1 MILE)

Explore stunning badlands formations below the Painted Canyon Visitor Center on this 1-mile loop trail. The trail proceeds 244 feet downhill to the canyon floor. The well-marked trail features steps and small bridges to assist the hiker. No dogs are allowed. You will not be disappointed with what you see along the way.

The trailhead is just west of the visitor center, near the picnic shelters. It is marked with a sign. On the descent, the trail passes through a grove of green ash trees. Woodsy areas like this one often are found on north facing slopes in the badlands. Then the trail enters a more open, rugged area. Go right at the Y in the trail. When we hiked in November, we noticed many bison tracks and buffalo pies on the trail and spotted a few bison in the distance.

By taking a side trail, you'll soon get a chance to climb a small badlands knoll that provides excellent views of the many different sediment layers that make up these badland formations. As you proceed, you'll see native prairie grasslands with sagebrush intermingled with wooded areas of Rocky Mountain juniper trees. The eroded sandstone in this area has the appearance of softly folded draperies.

Soon the trail starts uphill, across several small knolls. Be sure to turn around and look at the badlands scenery as you climb the slopes. The sun and clouds constantly create new colors and patterns on the landscape below.

QUESTIONS?

~ Theodore Roosevelt National Park, 701.623.4466; www.nps.gov/thro

LITTLE MISSOURI STATE PARK
BOB'S LOOP

What *makes this hike spectacular?* This challenging loop trail combines segments of the Thor, Travois and Indian trails and provides grand prospects of the Little Missouri River Valley and Little Missouri badlands. You'll hike along tall badlands ridges, take switchbacks past unusual geological formations and wind past Rocky Mountain juniper and through native prairie meadows dotted with wildflowers. Part of the trail is along a hogsback that allows you to see down both sides of the ridge and for miles in either direction. On a clear day you truly can see forever.

AT A GLANCE
BOB'S LOOP

Map:	**Page 86**
Location:	**Little Missouri State Park**
Nearest town:	**Killdeer**
Length:	**5 miles round trip.**
Elevation change:	**550 feet**
Dogs:	**Allowed on leashes**
Fees:	**Park entrance fee**
Services at trailhead:	**Ranger station and vault toilets**
Special notes:	**Trail hazardous when wet. The park is closed Nov. 1 to April 30.**

DIRECTIONS TO TRAILHEAD

Little Missouri State Park is 17 miles north of Killdeer on Highway 22. To find the trailhead, go to the north end of the campground, where a short (0.33 mile) road leads to several trailheads. Bob's Loop begins at Thor Trailhead. There is a parking area at the trailhead.

SUSAN'S NOTES ON THE HIKE

This 4,500-acre state park is located in a rugged section of the North Dakota badlands. Frequented by regional horseback riders, the trails are well marked, but occasionally rutted due to horse traffic. It is a challenging trail, with steep accents and descents, but if you take your time you will be rewarded with a terrific hiking experience.

The hike starts with marvelous views of the Little Missouri River Valley. In the first mile, Thor Trail descends about 400 feet from the top of the plateau down to a dry creek bed and native short-grass prairie.

The trail follows the edge of a badlands ridge twisting and turning north, west, east and south. As you make the turns, notice how the north-facing slopes along the ridge are covered with Rocky Mountain juniper, while the south-facing slopes are nearly bare of vegetation. Also, observe how soil colors change from dull grey to rose red. The red soil is the result of clay being baked by underground fires. As you approach the bottom of the ridge, you will see interesting sandstone formations created when softer layers of the porous rock eroded faster than harder layers.

Approximately 1.5 miles into the hike you will see a lightly used horse path leading to a gate. Do not follow this path. Stay on Thor's Trail, following a dry creek bed. You will cross the creek bed on a small wood bridge and pass through a stand of wild plum trees and groves of quaking aspen. When Bob, Sandy and I took this trail in late May, the wild plums were in bloom.

Keep hiking northward and pass through the gate shown on the map. Within 0.25 mile you will find a Travois Trail marker and another gate to pass through. Travois Trail heads east for 0.33 mile and then turns south and begins to ascend out of the valley. When we hiked here, this section of the trail was full of blooming wild-flowers. At first the climb is gradual, but when you join Hog Back Trail the trail steepens. Within 0.5 mile, you'll ascend about 300 feet. It's a challenge, but take your time, stop, rest and enjoy the spectacular scenery in every direction. Near the top you'll be trav-elling on the crest of a ridge with a slight slump, or hogsback and you feel like you are on top of the world.

Watch for the intersection with Indian Trail. You want to turn west to complete the loop back to your car. As you look west you can see the Killdeer Mountains. The hike now starts downhill again to cross to the plateau where the campground and your car are located. This descent is steep and requires careful footwork. The trail proceeds along the sides of ridges for about 0.5 mile before the final steep ascent to the edge of the plateau. The final portion of the hike offers grand views across the whole valley.

SANDY'S NOTES ON THE HIKE

I wore my dog backpack so I could carry my own water and a can-vas water bowl. The bowl enables me to drink every drop of water I carry. It was the first time I wore a backpack and I tried to bite the straps, but pretty soon I was so interested in the smells of the trail I forgot about it.

WHAT'S FOR LUNCH?

Before we started the hike, Bob and I enjoyed a lunch of cold fried chicken, rolls, coleslaw, pears and chocolate cake in the Little Missouri State Park picnic ground/campground. Killdeer, 19 miles south, is the closest town to pick up picnic supplies or purchase lunch.

ANOTHER FAVORITE HIKE

LITTLE MISSOURI STATE PARK
TRAVOIS TRAIL (1.5 MILES)

Little Missouri State Park has 48 miles of hiking trails. One of my favorite short hikes in the park is this 1.5-mile, nearly level segment of Travois Trail. This round-trip hike along a badland's ridge overlooks the scenic Little Missouri River Valley. Stop at the ranger station for a map of all the hiking trails in the park.

To find the trailhead, go to the north end of the campground and follow a short (0.33 mile) road until you find several trailheads. The Travois Trail (T) is on your left and heads west. Leashed dogs are allowed.

Although the trail loses about 50 feet of elevation at the start, most of the hike follows an almost-flat ridge. Rocky Mountain juniper and green ash woodlands, interspersed with short stretches of prairie, provide shade along the trail. The Little Missouri River lies approximately 2.5 miles to the north and badland's formations dominate the valley below. Walk along the Travois Trail 0.75 mile until you come to the intersection with the Shady Lane Trail (SL) and then turn around. The scenery is just as spectacular on the way back.

QUESTIONS?

~ Little Missouri State Park, 701.764.5256, www.parkrec.nd.gov/parks/lmbsp.htm

~ Horse Concession and Guide Service: 701.764.8000.

LITTLE MISSOURI NATIONAL GRASSLAND
SUMMIT TRAIL

What makes this hike spectacular? This hike combines vast views from a high, badlands plateau; an exciting walk along a 200-foot canyon wall; juniper forests, including the state's largest Rocky Mountain juniper; and finishes near the rugged hillsides of Theodore Roosevelt National Park's North Unit. Although it begins near Highway 85, this hike provides a wonderful backcountry experience.

AT A GLANCE

SUMMIT TRAIL

Map:	Page 87
Location:	Summit Campground, Little Missouri National Grassland
Nearest town:	Watford City
Length:	7 miles one way
Elevation change:	540 feet
Dogs:	Allowed
Fees:	None
Services at trailhead:	Information sign, vault toilets
Special notes:	Trail hazardous when wet. Also, you will need to arrange transportation from the endpoint of the hike in the CCC campground back to the trailhead in Summit Campground.
Hunting alert:	Avoid hiking here during hunting seasons

DIRECTIONS TO THE TRAILHEAD

Summit Campground, in the Little Missouri National Grassland, is 19 miles south of Watford City on Highway 85. The trail starts near the Summit Campground information sign. Wood posts bearing a mountain symbol mark Summit Trail, which leads toward the southwest.

SUSAN'S NOTES ON THE HIKE

Little Missouri National Grassland is the largest national grassland in the United States. Established in the 1930s, the grassland encompasses more than 1 million acres of land in western North Dakota and is managed by the U.S. Forest Service.

Summit Trail is in a rugged, scenic section of the national grassland. The 7-mile hike starts at Summit Campground and ends at the CCC campground. Therefore, you'll need to arrange transportation back to the trailhead. Leashing is not required, but dogs need to be under control. Leashes will be helpful if you encounter cattle, riders on horseback, bicycle riders, etc.

The trail begins in high-country meadows, where wildflowers dazzle in the spring and cattle graze after the first of June. If the cattle get in your way, just yell and clap your hands and they'll step aside. The gently rolling trail is adjacent to deep badlands canyons, so the scenery is wonderful, but keep an eye on children and pets.

The next section of the trail, about 1.5 miles from the start, isn't for the faint of heart. You'll enter a Rocky Mountain juniper forest, pass through a gate and cross a high ridge called a hogsback. The path is narrow, but provides excellent, close-up views of the deep canyons on each side. If you're vigilant you may see a bighorn sheep, but they're tough to spot because they blend in with the rocky slopes. You'll descend toward the canyon floor via about 0.75 miles of switchbacks. This is the most dramatic section of the trail, and the most exciting. There are 200-foot drop-offs next to the trail, so children and pets must be carefully watched.

Continuing toward the canyon floor, you'll enter a Rocky Mountain juniper forest and grassy meadows. The trail crosses a nearly dry creek bed and gradually heads upward around a ridge and through another juniper forest in which you'll find North Dakota's largest Rocky Mountain juniper. Its diameter measures 29 inches.

Bob, Sandy and I didn't see much wildlife on our hike, but we did hear a number of birds and encountered a large bullsnake on the trail. We took its picture and then walked around it. Bullsnakes' scales are gold, tan and black and their tails don't have rattles.

The trail continues downhill and near milepost 94 meets the Maah Daah Hey Trail, which you follow for the next 2 miles to the CCC campground. This portion of the Maah Daah Hey Trail follows a dry creek bed for 1 mile. It then traverses gently rolling hills, providing beautiful views across the Little Missouri River of Theodore Roosevelt National Park's North Unit, where we saw a herd of bison grazing on a hillside.

SANDY'S NOTES ON THE HIKE

When Susan and Bob sat down for a short break along the trail, I decided to roll around in the soft grass with my backpack on. Bob became alarmed and rushed to grab my leash, because I was getting too close to the edge of a high cliff. Even in May the streams along the trail were mostly dry, so I drank every drop of the two quarts of water I carried with me. And while the mud along the streambeds was deep and cool, Susan wouldn't let me take a rest there.

WHAT'S FOR LUNCH?

Today we lunched on sliced, cold grilled steak on rolls, fresh tomato and cucumber slices, and potato chips. For dessert and for snacking along the trail we brought along apples, apricots and trail mix. If you want to purchase picnic food or meals, Watford City, 19 miles north of the Summit Campground, has several restaurants and a grocery store.

SUMMIT TRAIL (3-MILE, ROUND-TRIP VERSION)

This is a shorter version of the Summit Trail Hike. It also starts at Summit Campground, but this 3-mile, round-trip hike is on gently rolling terrain and stays on the grassy plateau high above the badland canyons. About 1.5 miles from the trailhead you'll enter a Rocky Mountain juniper woodland and see a gate, which is the hike's turnaround point.

QUESTIONS?

~ Dakota Prairie Grasslands, 701.250.4443, www.fs.fed.us/r1/dakotaprairie

BENNETT TRAIL

What *makes this hike spectacular?* **Bennett Creek winds through a broad badlands valley where the surrounding, colorful ridges provide gorgeous views. The trail generally follows the slopes above the valley floor, but you'll also cross Bennett Creek gully and explore other side canyons. You'll traverse grassy slumps at the base of badlands buttes, where Rocky Mountain juniper trees, clumps of sage, wildflowers, native fruit trees and bushes grow among native prairie grasses.**

DIRECTIONS TO TRAILHEAD

To find Bennett Creek Campground, Little Missouri National Grassland, drive 17 miles south of Watford City on Highway 85. Turn west on Bennett Creek Road and travel 4 miles west. Watch for pronghorn (locally known as antelope) along this road. At the sign directing you to Bennett Campground turn left (south) and travel 1.5 miles. Bennett trailhead is near the campground entrance, next to a bee hive-shaped badlands formation. You'll find a parking area several hundred feet from the trailhead. The trail is marked with wood posts imprinted with the image of a ram's head.

AT A GLANCE

BENNETT TRAIL

Map:	**Page 88**
Location:	**Bennett Campground, Little Missouri National Grassland**
Nearest town:	**Watford City**
Length:	**4 miles round trip**
Elevation change:	**75 feet**
Entrance Fee:	**None**
Dogs:	**Allowed**
Fees:	**None**
Services at trailhead:	**Information sign, vault toilets**
Special notes:	**Trail hazardous when wet**
Hunting alert:	**Avoid hiking here during hunting seasons**

SUSAN'S NOTES ON THE HIKE

Little Missouri National Grassland is the largest national grassland in the United States, encompassing more than 1 million acres in western North Dakota. The grassland contains areas of gently rolling prairie grasslands and rugged badlands. Bennett Trail is in a scenic, badlands section of the national grassland.

Dogs do not need to be leashed, but need to be under control. Leashes will be helpful if you encounter cattle, riders on horseback, bicycle riders or other hikers.

Bob, Sandy and I hiked this trail in late May. The trail crosses Bennett Creek a short distance from the trailhead. There is no bridge, but at the time there was only about six inches of water flowing through the creek bed so, although our shoes got wet, crossing was easy. Of course, Sandy waded on through, stopping to get a drink in the cool water. This is the only creek crossing on this hike. Following heavy rains it can carry quite a bit of water.

After crossing Bennett Creek, the trail winds gently up and around grassy slopes created by years of erosion on the badland ridges all around you. After about 0.5 mile on the trail you will encounter a canyon washout area that contains unusual clay columns and a small cave.

As you meander along the trail, notice how many different bushes, trees and plants are present in this native prairie environment. Also, look for the different layers in each of the badland ridges. The black layers are lignite coal and the grey layers are clay, formed from volcanic ash deposited millions of years ago.

About 1 mile up the trail you will come to a scenic location where a trail post serves as a memorial to a bicyclist who once rode the Maah Daah Hey Trail. Killed in traffic in Chicago, the man's family dedicated this post to him, because his first name was Bennett.

The trail continues along the hillside and then descends into Bennett Creek gully. Ranging from 15 to 30 feet deep and quite wide in places, the gully has the capacity to carry lots of water but at the end of May the creek was only a few inches deep. Do not cross Bennett Creek. Cross a box canyon that runs into Bennett Creek and then proceed up grassy slopes along the badland's ridges. For the 4-mile round-trip hike, turn around about 0.5 mile farther up the trail where the valley broadens and the trail enters an area of sagebrush flats. If you're up for a longer hike, Bennett Trail continues west 0.5 miles and then joins the Maah Daah Hey Trail.

I always enjoy hiking back the way I came in the badlands, because everything looks different and I get to enjoy my favorite spots one more time.

SANDY'S NOTES ON THE HIKE

Crossing Bennett Creek was no problem for me. I love getting my feet wet.

WHAT'S FOR LUNCH?

We left our cooler in the car and ate a tasty salad when we returned to the campground. Before the hike I mixed cold, sliced beef and some Italian salad dressing in a plastic bag. In another plastic bag I placed ready-to-eat salad greens, sliced cucumber and sliced peppers. Both of these bags went into the cooler. At picnic time, I mixed the contents of the two bags and, voilà, lunch was ready. Buttered rolls, chocolate bars and fresh apricots completed our meal. The closest grocery store is in Watford City, 22 miles away, so plan carefully.

QUESTIONS?

~ Dakota Prairie Grasslands, 701.250.4443, www.fs.fed.us/r1/dakotaprairie

KATE'S WALK ON THE MAAH DAAH HEY TRAIL

What makes this hike spectacular? At 2,650 feet, this section of the Maah Daah Hey Trail features one of the highest elevations on the 96-mile long trail and provides panoramic views of the Killdeer Mountains, buttes and badlands ridges. Kate's Walk starts at a high elevation, so to reach this marvelous viewpoint you need climb only 75 feet. The trail also features a beautiful woody draw with a small pond. The turnaround point is at an outstanding place to see miles of rugged badlands ridges and canyons.

AT A GLANCE
KATE'S WALK

Map:	Page 89
Location:	Little Missouri National Grassland
Nearest town:	Grassy Butte
Length:	3 miles round trip
Elevation change:	125 feet
Entrance fee:	None
Dogs:	Allowed
Fees:	None
Services at trailhead:	None
Special notes:	Trail hazardous when wet
Hunting alert:	Avoid hiking here during hunting seasons

DIRECTIONS TO TRAILHEAD

The trailhead for this section of the Maah Daah Hey Trail is 5.5 miles west of Grassy Butte on Beiceigel Road (County Road 50). Beiceigel Road is a paved road leading west, just north of the small town of Grassy Butte. After you travel west on Beiceigel Road for 5.5 miles, watch for a sign indicating a horse crossing and a wood marker on the north side of the road, part way up the hill. This is where you pick up the trail for this hike. Pull off the road and park your car.

SUSAN'S NOTES ON THE HIKE

Many of us will never be able to hike the entire 96-mile – and growing – Maah Daah Hey Trail, but at 3 miles Kate's Walk offers a chance to experience the Maah Daah Hey. It's an easy hike and perfect for a family outing. Our daughter Kate chose this section of the trail to introduce her husband, Rob, to badlands hiking.

Dogs do not need to be leashed, but need to be under control. Leashes will be helpful if you encounter cattle, riders on horseback, bicycle riders or other hikers.

Within a few minutes of starting the hike you'll be standing on one of the highest spots on the Maah Daah Hey Trail. On a clear, spring evening, we could see the Killdeer Mountains 20 miles to the east, badlands ridges along the Little Missouri River 20 miles to the north, and distant vistas to the south and west.

In late May, the grassy, native-prairie ridge was covered with wild-flowers. This land is a section of North Dakota State School Land. When North Dakota became a state in 1889, the federal government gave North Dakota state school land. Income generated by selling or leasing this land goes into a common trust fund for schools.

Just beyond milepost 73 – every mile of Maah Daah Hey Trail is marked – the trail descends into a woody draw, lush with green ash, chokecherry and shrubs. Damming on a small stream has formed a small pond, creating an unexpected, woodsy dell environment. It's not surprising we saw several mule deer here.

When you come upon a state school land sign, you'll know a patch of badlands lies ahead. The trail proceeds through rough, eroded banks; switches back and forth up the hillside through a wooded area; and continues through native prairie. At milepost 74, you'll reach a grassy knoll with an awesome vista of the badlands. This is the turnaround point for the 3-mile, round-trip hike and is a wonderful place to linger for a picnic lunch or a snack.

For constant views of the canyons and ridges to the west, continue hiking through the broad, native-prairie meadows to milepost 75. This extension turns Kate's Walk into a 5-mile, round-trip hike and we highly recommend it.

SANDY'S NOTES ON THE HIKE

We had a sudden shower near the end of the hike and when the wind tore Bob's plastic rain jacket as he unfolded it, he got pretty excited. Bob knows how slippery it gets in the badlands when it rains. Fortunately, we only had a quarter mile more to hike. I don't mind getting muddy and wet, but we were all glad to get to the car.

WHAT'S FOR LUNCH?

Today we carried our lunch in a small daypack so we could eat on the trail. We brought along cheese, crackers, apples, hummus, beef jerky sticks, oatmeal cookies, juice packs, wine and a corkscrew. Perfect lunch spots are plentiful on this hike. We ate on a grassy ridge overlooking the scenic badlands. Watford City, 27 miles northeast, has a grocery store for picnic supplies and several restaurants.

QUESTIONS?

~ Dakota Prairie Grasslands, 701.250.4443; www.fs.fed.us/r1/dakotaprairie

THEODORE ROOSEVELT NATIONAL PARK – NORTH UNIT
TRAIL TO SPERATI POINT

What makes this hike spectacular? **When you want to take a short hike that gives you a feeling of the vastness of the western North Dakota prairies, this is the one. The prairie landscape extends to the horizon. Since this hike is along the top of the ridges of the breathtaking Little Missouri River Valley, it includes superb views of the valley flanked by the rugged, colorful badlands. The pristine native prairie along the trail contains hundreds of grasses, wildflowers and other prairie plants. And you may see bison.**

AT A GLANCE

TRAIL TO SPERATI POINT

Map:	Page 90
Location:	Theodore Roosevelt National Park – North Unit
Nearest town:	Watford City
Length:	1.5 miles round trip
Elevation change:	150 feet
Dogs:	No dogs allowed on trails
Fees:	Park entrance fee
Services at trailhead:	None
Special notes:	Trail access closed early November to mid-March

DIRECTIONS TO THE TRAILHEAD

Theodore Roosevelt National Park's North Unit is 14 miles south of Watford City on Highway 85. The trail to Sperati Point starts at the end of a 14-mile scenic drive through the park. You'll find a parking area adjacent to Oxbow Overlook. The trailhead is near the southwest corner of the parking area. A trail register and sign for Achenbach Trail indicates Sperati Point is 0.7 mile along the 18-mile Achenbach Trail.

SUSAN'S NOTES ON THE HIKE

With its opportunities to see wildlife, interesting badlands formations and interpretive signs about human and geologic history, the drive to Oxbow Overlook is lovely. And Oxbow Overlook offers stunning views of the Little Missouri River Valley, but the view at Sperati Point is even better.

As you start the hike, take a close look at the native prairie along the trail. Although I saw no bison on the day I took this hike, an abundance of buffalo pies mean bison graze here. Grazing is nature's way of managing the land and is good for the prairie. Bison eat cool-weather grasses in the spring, which allows the sun to mature warm-weather grasses, which bison will eat later in the summer. You will see some grasses are eaten down to the ground, while others are left standing. When grass is plentiful, bison (and cattle) have their favorites – nicknamed ice cream grasses – which they eat first.

The mat of grasses and forbs or wildflowers appears tough, and it is. The roots of these perennial plants reach deep into the soil for moisture and endure temperatures ranging from 40-below zero to 115 degrees above. Droughts can last for months and then it might rain several inches in a few days.

I took this hike in mid-May, after a few days of heavy rain. The grass was green, I saw at least five species of wildflowers in bloom, and – because the prairie had absorbed every bit of moisture – the trails were mud free. The trail is marked with wood posts, which the bison have adopted as scratching posts, leaving telltale tufts behind.

The prairie trail winds along small slopes, with interesting rock outcrops. Low-growing creeping juniper hugs the north-facing hillsides. Since this is a prairie hike, the trail stays out in the open spaces, but there are several woody draws near the trail. Some of these lead down the steep, badlands slopes of the Little Missouri River Valley. In mid-May the new quaking aspen leaves in the woody draws were a fresh yellow green, which provided a nice contrast to the dark color of the Rocky Mountain juniper.

The trail proceeds up a gentle slope near the edge of the valley, offering long views of the river far below. Continuing along the trail, I scared up a dozen grouse. At the top of the rise, you'll see a marker with an arrow that says: Sperati Point .1 mile. Now the trail leads slightly downhill to Sperati Point, a grassy area with superb views of the Little Missouri Valley to the east and south.

Rugged, 500-foot badland ridges surround the broad river valley. For more than 500,000 years water, wind and weather have shaped the badlands. The river cuts a lazy S-curve through the lightly wooded valley where eastern cottonwood trees flourish. This is one of the most beautiful views in North Dakota. From this point, Achenbach Trail leads steeply downhill into the valley, so unless you want to continue on a more rugged hike, this is the place to turn back toward the trailhead.

SANDY'S NOTES ON THE HIKE

Dogs are not allowed on National Park trails so Susan left me at home.

WHAT'S FOR LUNCH?

Bob and I chose to have our lunch at Sperati Point. Our meal of boiled eggs, buttered banana bread, orange and apple slices and coconut-chocolate bars tasted great while we watched the river winding below us. If you prefer to eat in a shady spot with picnic tables and restrooms, stop at Juniper Campground and Picnic Area along the scenic drive. Watford City 14 miles north of the park entrance, has a grocery store for picnic supplies and several restaurants.

OTHER HIKES IN THE PARK

Theodore Roosevelt National Park – North Unit has many miles of hiking trails of varying difficulty and length. Visitor Center and some trailheads are open year round. Stop at the park entrance station for current trail conditions and information. Dogs may not be left unattended in vehicles.

QUESTIONS?

～ Theodore Roosevelt National Park – North Unit, 701.842.2333; www.nps.gov/thro

We were alert for bison — commonly known as buffalo — and while we didn't see any on this hike, we did spy many, fresh buffalo pies.

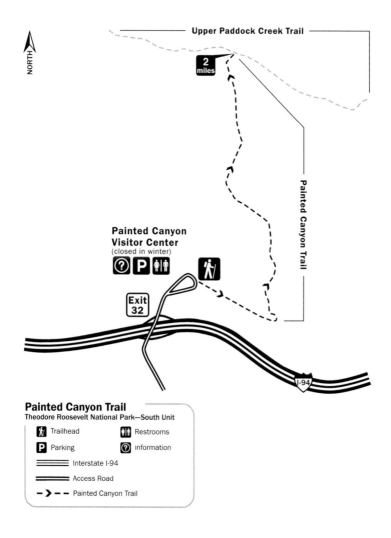

Upper Paddock Creek Trail

2 miles

NORTH

Painted Canyon Trail

Painted Canyon
Visitor Center
(closed in winter)

Exit 32

I-94

Painted Canyon Trail
Theodore Roosevelt National Park—South Unit

🚶 Trailhead		🚻 Restrooms	
🅿 Parking		❓ Information	
═══ Interstate I-94			
═══ Access Road			
➤ Painted Canyon Trail			

Want to know more about this trail?
TURN TO PAGE 62

You will cross the creek bed on a small wood bridge and pass through a stand of wild plum trees and groves of quaking aspen.

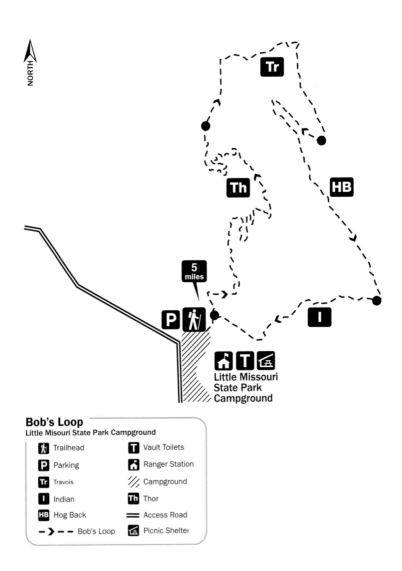

Bob's Loop
Little Misouri State Park Campground

Trailhead		Vault Toilets	
Parking		Ranger Station	
Travois		Campground	
Indian		Thor	
Hog Back		Access Road	
Bob's Loop		Picnic Shelter	

Want to know more about this trail?

TURN TO PAGE 67

The path is narrow, but provides excellent, close-up views of the deep canyons on each side.

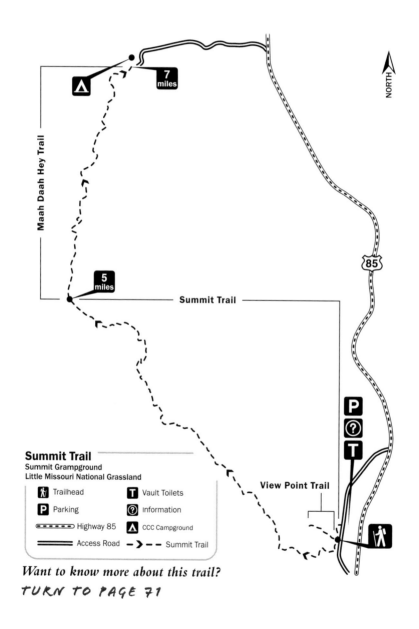

Summit Trail
Summit Grampground
Little Missouri National Grassland

🚶 Trailhead		🅣 Vault Toilets	
🅿 Parking		❓ Information	
▪▪▪▪▪ Highway 85		🔺 CCC Campground	
═══ Access Road		➤ – Summit Trail	

Want to know more about this trail?

TURN TO PAGE 71

After crossing Bennett Creek, the trail winds gently up and around grassy slopes created by years of erosion on the badland ridges all around you.

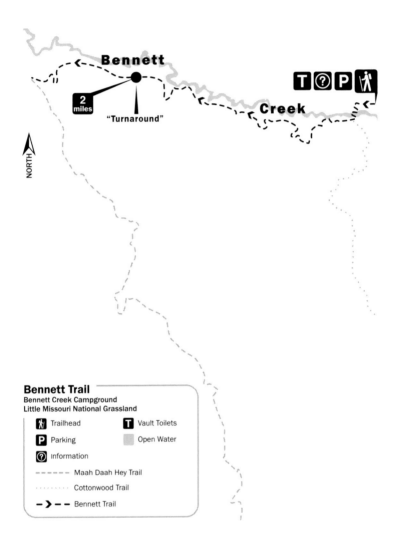

Bennett Trail
Bennett Creek Campground
Little Missouri National Grassland

🧍 Trailhead		🅃 Vault Toilets	
🅿 Parking		⬜ Open Water	
⑦ Information			
- - - - - Maah Daah Hey Trail			
· · · · · · · Cottonwood Trail			
—➤— — Bennett Trail			

Want to know more about this trail?
TURN TO PAGE 74

Within a few minutes of starting the hike you will be standing on one of the highest spots on the Maah Daah Hey Trail.

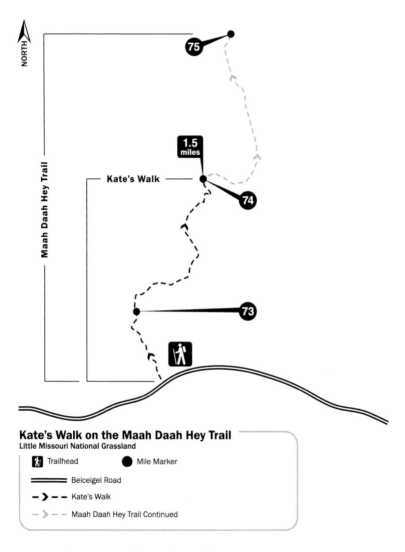

Kate's Walk on the Maah Daah Hey Trail
Little Missouri National Grassland

- Trailhead
- Mile Marker
- Beiceigel Road
- Kate's Walk
- Maah Daah Hey Trail Continued

Want to know more about this trail?
TURN TO PAGE 77

The trail is marked with wood posts, which the bison have adopted as scratching posts, leaving telltale tufts behind.

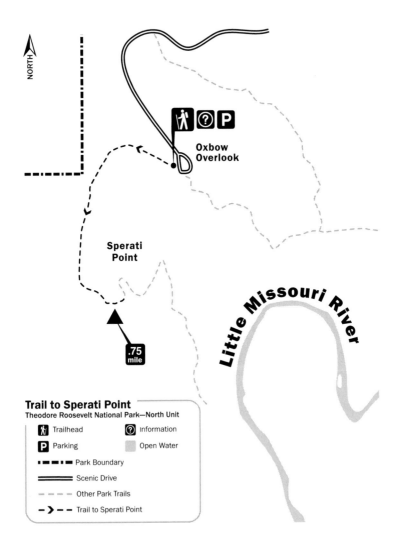

Oxbow
Overlook

Sperati
Point

Little Missouri River

.75
mile

Trail to Sperati Point
Theodore Roosevelt National Park—North Unit

🏃 Trailhead		⑦ Information	
🅿 Parking		▨ Open Water	
▪ ▬ ▪ ▬ Park Boundary			
▬▬▬ Scenic Drive			
- - - - Other Park Trails			
- ❯ - - Trail to Sperati Point			

Want to know more about this trail?
TURN TO PAGE 81

MY NOTES

FIVE

PRAIRIE RIVERS
OF THE NORTHEAST

> Green branches
> Arching grandly above prairie rivers
> Remind me of arching altar alcoves
> In small prairie churches.
> — Susan Wefald

AREA ATTRACTIONS

Larimore Dam Campground and Recreation Area is a great place to swim and cool off on a summer day. Larimore Golf Club is adjacent to the recreation area.

~ Grand Forks Air Force Base, 3 miles east of Turtle River State Park, has restored aircraft on display near the front gate.

~ Pembina County Historical Museum and Pioneer Machinery Grounds, across the road from Icelandic State Park, is a treasure house of artifacts from pioneer days.

WHERE TO HIKE

- *Turtle River State Park, Larimore*
- *Icelandic State Park, Cavalier*
- *Greater Grand Forks Greenway, Grand Forks*
- *University of North Dakota Campus, Grand Forks*

~ The Pioneer Heritage Center at Icelandic State Park has interesting exhibits on the life of settlers from 1870 to 1920.

~ Wind farms are used generate electricity throughout North Dakota. You'll find a large wind farm near Langdon, 20 miles west of Icelandic State Park.

~ The University of North Dakota, Grand Forks, has a beautiful campus and offers a full calendar of cultural, athletic and educational events.

~ The North Dakota Museum of Art, on the UND campus, has three galleries filled with regional, national and international art.

~ The North Dakota Mill and Elevator – the only state-owned mill in the United States – turns North Dakota wheat into flour. Tours are available, but must be arranged in advance. The mill is in Grand Forks.

~ The Japanese Garden in Grand Forks' Sertoma Park is worth exploring.

AREA ACCOMMODATIONS

~ Turtle River State Park has a shady campground and 6 rustic cabins for rent.

~ Larimore Dam Campground and Recreation Area has a large campground and other recreation facilities.

~ Icelandic State Park has a pleasant campground.

~ The cities of Grand Forks, Grafton and Cavalier all offer a variety of lodging options.

TURTLE RIVER STATE PARK
TURTLE RIVER FOREST LOOP

What makes this hike spectacular? **Northeastern North Dakota's Turtle River State Park is a perfect example of the power of even a small river to transform prairie into woodlands. As you hike beside the meandering Turtle River, you'll see for yourself how abruptly the riparian forest – with its huge ironwood and basswood trees – gives way to grasslands. Turtle River State Park also is home to classic structures built by the Civilian Conservation Corp between 1934 and 1942. Plus, the state stocks the river with rainbow trout, so bring your fly rod.**

DIRECTIONS TO TRAILHEAD

Turtle River State Park is 22 miles west of Grand Forks on Highway 2. After entering the park, follow signs to Woodland Lodge and park on the river side of the lodge parking lot. Cross the bridge directly south of the lodge. Immediately after crossing the bridge you will see the trailhead on your right. During my visit to the park, this trail was well maintained, but not well signed. Be sure to consult the map and carefully watch for trail intersections.

AT A GLANCE
TURTLE RIVER FOREST LOOP

Map:	**Page 106**
Location:	**Turtle River State Park**
Nearest town:	**Grand Forks**
Length:	**3-mile loop**
Elevation change:	**Less than 50 feet**
Dogs:	**Allowed on leashes**
Fees:	**Park entrance fee**
Services at trailhead:	**None**

SUSAN'S NOTES ON THE HIKE

The people of North Dakota realized early on that wooded area along the Turtle River was special. Riparian zones like this one provide excellent environment for wildlife, enhance water quality and make pleasant places for human recreation. In 1934, the State of North Dakota created one of its first state parks by purchasing 475 acres of State School Land along the Turtle River.

The timing was perfect for the state to take advantage of federal legislation creating the Civilian Conservation Corps. The CCC put Depression-era laborers to work on public projects across the country and Turtle River State Park greatly benefited. Many CCC-constructed buildings, picnic shelters, bridges, roads and trails are still in use today, including the park's beautiful Woodland Lodge. The lodge is so highly valued, when a massive flood damaged it in 2000, the entire structure was dismantled piece by piece and moved to higher ground. The huge stone fireplace still stands on the 1937 building site.

Turtle River Forest Loop combines segments of several summer trails on the west side of the park into a 3.0-mile loop trail. (The park's winter trail map features different trails.) The first part of the hike follows a marked nature trail along the Turtle River through a open woodland of American basswood, green ash and bur oak.

Across the river you'll see Memorial Picnic Shelter. Another vintage CCC structure, it was built in 1937 as a bathhouse for the swimming pond the CCC created by damming the river. Swimming is no longer allowed in the river, but the small stone dam is still in place.

When the nature trail turns up the hill, away from the river, do not follow it. Continue hiking straight ahead and soon you will be hiking on a small ridge about 30 feet above the river. When I hiked here in early June, the setting was idyllic: yellow, purple and white violets were blooming along the trail, the river was slowly flowing and the birds were singing in the trees. The trail follows the river deeper into the woods and at a place where a small sandbar had formed, I stopped to enjoy the sounds and smells of the forest and the river and to eat a snack.

The trail continues through the river bottomlands. Filled with American basswood, bur oak, green ash and ironwood (eastern hop horn beam), this is a wonderful place to take your time and look for deer tracks and signs of other animals. As you hike through this shady, damp part of the forest, it's difficult to imagine sunny prairieland lies just over the ridge.

This part of the trail makes a large loop through the forest. To avoid hiking the same loop twice, be sure to watch for the trail on the right. I had this problem, but soon realized my error and corrected my mistake by turning around and following the river a short distance downstream. From here, you rejoin the nature trail and head up the hill. This part of the trail passes through a transition zone between forest and prairie. Here I saw clusters of hawthorn and thickets of chokecherry trees and several white-tailed deer grazing in a grassy area.

The nature trail crosses a small ravine and leads up to a small section of prairie. Park rangers occasionally conduct controlled burns here to keep the forest from spilling over into the prairie. Bluebird houses have been installed to encourage nesting. I didn't see any bluebirds, but I did see many swallows. Follow the path along the north edge of the prairie, where the prairie grasses meet the bur oak trees of the woodland.

Soon you will come to an old road, which leads to the left, down toward the river. Take this road back to the bridge and the start of the hike.

SANDY'S NOTES ON THE HIKE

Susan had meetings in Grand Forks and did not take me on this hike.

WHAT'S FOR LUNCH?

I packed my lunch and left it in the car so it would be ready when I returned from my hike. I enjoyed my simple meal – vacuum-packed lemon-pepper tuna, dinner rolls, a fresh tomato, potato chips and a beverage – in Hillside Picnic Area. This shady picnic spot, located on the main park road about 0.25 mile from the trailhead, has two charming CCC-era picnic shelters and several grills. You'll find lavatories here too. If you wish to purchase lunch, consider driving 7 miles southwest to the Larimore Country Club or 22 miles east to Grand Forks, where you'll find numerous restaurants.

OTHER HIKES IN THE PARK

Turtle River State Park has several places to hike. Check at the park office for a map of all the trails.

QUESTIONS?

~ Turtle River State Park, 701.594.4445, www.parkrec.nd.gov/parks/trsp.htm

ICELANDIC STATE PARK
SHADY SPRINGS TRAIL

What makes this hike spectacular? Icelandic State Park is home to Gunlogson State Nature Preserve, where rare plant and bird species are protected. Shady Springs Trail winds through a spring-filled area of the preserve along the Tongue River. The moist ground is covered with scouring rushes, a plant that has been around for millions of years. Large trees and ferns are everywhere. In this magical place, you might expect to see a fairy or a gnome perched on a tree branch.

AT A GLANCE
SHADY SPRINGS TRAIL

Map:	**Page 107**
Location:	**Icelandic State Park**
Nearest town:	**Cavalier**
Length:	**0.75-mile loop**
Elevation change:	**less than 50 feet**
Dogs:	**No dogs allowed**
Fees:	**Park entrance fee**
Services at trailhead:	**Pioneer Heritage Center with lavatories**

DIRECTIONS TO TRAILHEAD

Icelandic State Park is 5 miles west of Cavalier on Highway 5. The trailhead for all trails is behind Pioneer Heritage Center, which doubles as park headquarters. Trail maps and a brochure for Wildwood Nature Trail are available in the center or at the trailhead. To find the start of Shady Springs Trail, hike 0.25 mile from the Wildwood Trail trailhead marker.

SUSAN'S NOTES ON THE HIKE

G.B. Gunlogson loved the forested, spring-filled land along the Tongue River. In 1963 he donated his home and 200 acres to the state, allowing visitors to experience this lush woodlands much as early settlers did when they arrived in the 1880s.

Before you set off on Shady Springs Trail, I suggest you tour Pioneer Heritage Center. Ask the center staff for keys and a brochure and at the end of your hike you will be ready to tour Gunlogson Homestead and the other historic buildings.

At first I wasn't going to take Shady Springs Trail. My day was ending and I had just finished hiking Settlers Trail (see Another Favorite Hike). However, as soon as I started walking, I became entranced by what a friend of mine calls a fen. I like that word. Fen sounds much more magical than bog or swamp. The beautiful fen on the Shady Springs Trail is filled with large trees, ferns, rushes and springs, a perfect home for fairies or gnomes. Its one of several reasons I fell in love in with this trail.

First, I loved the way the trail winds through the springs area. Second, the trail is right along the river and in early June I loved seeing the contrasts of color and texture between the rushing river, the muddy riverbanks and the green of the scouring rushes and ferns.

The rushes are called scouring rushes because early settlers used them to scour their pots and pans. I've been fascinated by them ever since I was a little girl. I called them puzzle plants, because I would pick one, pull the segmented stems apart piece-by-piece and then try to put the pieces together again. Of course, in a state park I would never pick one of these plants.

I also loved this hike for its freshwater springs and shady environment, which allows rare North Dakota plants to live here. I enjoyed looking for unusual ferns and the showy lady's slipper, one of my favorite wildflowers. I lingered here for awhile, enchanted by my surroundings.

When I was ready to move on, I followed the trail up the bank out of the forest to the park's pioneer heritage buildings. As I gradually worked my way through the buildings, I enjoyed thinking about early settlers farming the land, raising their families and organizing churches, schools and civic groups. I especially enjoyed Hallson Church. Built in 1897, the church originally stood four miles west of the park.

SANDY'S NOTES ON THE HIKE

Dogs are not allowed on the trails in Gunlogson Nature Preserve and Homestead so I was left at home.

WHAT'S FOR LUNCH?

Today, at various sites along the trail, I munched on an apple, snack bars and almonds. If you've packed a less portable picnic, I recommend the picnic ground near the park swimming beach. Cavalier, 5 miles east, is the closest town to pick up picnic supplies or purchase lunch.

ANOTHER FAVORITE HIKE

ICELANDIC STATE PARK
SETTLERS TRAIL (3 MILES)

On the early June day I hiked here, the sun was shining, the new forest leaves were a soft green, and I thoroughly enjoyed exploring this beautiful part of Icelandic State Park. Settlers Trail passes through grassy meadows between stands of quaking aspen, paper birch and bur oak. It's a wide, grassy trail that follows the park's northern boundary. The 3-mile loop trail also includes sections of Wildwood Nature Trail and Basswood Trail.

This nearly level, loop trail starts at the main trailhead behind Pioneer Heritage Center. Maps are available at the visitor center. The trail is well marked and easy to follow. Dogs are not allowed.

Proceed south on the Wildwood Nature Trail, use the footbridge to cross the Tongue River, then turn right onto Basswood Trail. Basswood Trail has many American basswood trees and a dense, 6-foot-tall shrub layer composed of beaked hazel and American hazel. These hazel bushes produce edible hazelnuts in the fall. Along the river, I saw several tree stumps cut by beavers.

Basswood Trail connects with Settlers Trail, which rejoins Basswood Trail and leads back to the trailhead.

QUESTIONS?

~ Icelandic State Park, 701.265.4561, www.parkrec.nd.gov/parks/isp.htm

GREATER GRAND FORKS GREENWAY
DOWNTOWN RIVERFRONT WALK

What makes this hike spectacular? **In 1997, Grand Forks was devastated by a major Red River flood. Many parts of the city were destroyed by water and sections of the downtown were destroyed by fire. Today the 2,200-acre Greater Grand Forks Greenway helps protect Grand Forks and its sister city, East Grand Forks, Minn., from future floods. Bordering the Red and Red Lake rivers, the greenway is filled with trails and other recreational facilities. This hike highlights the Grand Forks riverfront and new downtown and includes a walk across Sorlie Memorial Bridge into Minnesota.**

AT A GLANCE

DOWNTOWN RIVERFRONT WALK

Map:	**Page 108**
Location:	**Greater Grand Forks Greenway**
Nearest town:	**Grand Forks**
Length:	**1.5-mile loop**
Elevation change:	**Less than 50 feet**
Dogs:	**Allowed on leashes**
Fees:	**None**
Services at trailhead:	**Information kiosk**

DIRECTIONS TO TRAILHEAD

This hike starts in downtown Grand Forks on Demers Avenue, next to Sorlie Memorial Bridge. You'll find parking next to the bridge, adjacent to Community Green Rotary Park and a Greater Grand Forks Greenway information kiosk nearby.

SUSAN'S NOTES ON THE HIKE

To start this hike, cross Demers Avenue and proceed south on the greenway trail along the Red River. Most times of the year it's difficult to imagine the placid river causing any damage, but in the spring this river carries a lot of runoff. In addition to the greenway, which was completed in 2007, you'll see earthen dikes and huge gates that now protect the two cities. A marker along the trail shows heights reached by floodwaters in past years.

Grand Forks is named for the place where the north-flowing Red River and Red Lake River come together. As you continue down the greenway path you'll see the place where the two rivers meet.

About 0.5 mile from the start of the hike, just after the Minnesota Bridge, leave the greenway trail and proceed up to Minnesota Avenue. You will see Kamnowski Park, a small park with a playground, information kiosk, water fountains and lavatories. Walk to Kamnowski Park and then cross the street and proceed north on 4th Street, heading toward downtown. You'll walk through an old neighborhood containing some charming houses built around 1900 and continue past the 1913 Grand Forks County Courthouse, a statue of Grand Forks founder Alexander Griggs and the new Grand Forks County Office Building, built after the 1997 flood. The courthouse is open to visitors during normal business hours.

As you continue down 4th Street, interpretive signs provide information on the mix of new and old buildings in this area. Between Kittson and Demers, you'll see a small park, with a gazebo and a sculpture garden. When you turn right onto Demers Avenue, walking toward Sorlie Memorial Bridge, you'll pass Grand Forks Town Square, a public gathering place with a small stage.

As you cross the 1929 bridge, think about the barges, flatboats and steamboats that once carried passengers and freight up and down the Red River. In the 1870s, it took a steamboat 60 hours to make the trip from Fargo to Winnipeg, Manitoba. Commercial traffic on the Red River ended when railroad lines were completed.

When you reach the end of the bridge you'll be in downtown East Grand Forks. Watch for traffic and then cross the street to the other side of the bridge and return across the river from Minnesota back into North Dakota.

SANDY'S NOTES ON THE HIKE

I didn't accompany Susan on this hike, because she had business in Grand Forks and left me at home.

WHAT'S FOR LUNCH?

Downtown Grand Forks has a number of inviting places to dine. One of my favorite spots along the hike route is the coffee shop on the corner of Kittson and 4th Street. When I walked here in June, I opted to sit at one of the shop's outdoor tables and enjoy the pleasant, warm day.

ANOTHER FAVORITE HIKE

UNIVERSITY OF NORTH DAKOTA
CAMPUS WALK (1 MILE)

The University of North Dakota, established in 1883 in Grand Forks, serves more than 14,000 students. The 549-acre campus is filled with colorful flowerbeds, historic buildings and tall shade trees. This loop hike takes you along English Coulee, a small stream that meanders through a beautiful section of the central campus, and includes a chance to visit the North Dakota Museum of Art.

The walk begins at the corner of Yale Drive and University Avenue, next to the President's house and across from Chester Fritz Auditorium. With seating for 2,300, The Fritz is the largest auditorium in the state. You will find public parking here. Leashed dogs are allowed.

Start the campus walk on the paved trail along English Coulee. Nearby is 1907 Adelphi Fountain, a picturesque area favored by campus photographers. After crossing Fox Memorial Bridge, you have the option of visiting the North Dakota Museum of Art, one-half block to your right. This popular contemporary art museum has a delightful outdoor sculpture garden and you'll find a public restaurant inside.

After visiting the museum, return to the paved path near Old Main Memorial Sphere, where an eternal flame burns. This path leads into one of the original campus squares. Proceed around the square to the area behind the Chester Fritz Library. There are lovely gardens here, including a prairie wildflower garden.

Proceeding west (to your left as you face the rear of the library) you will come to the front of Gamble Hall. Turn right here and head towards University Avenue. Soon you will pass the charming old president's house, now the Alumni Center, which you can tour with advance reservations. Turn left on University and follow this main street through the campus back to Chester Fritz Auditorium.

QUESTIONS?

~ City of Grand Forks, 701.746.2733;
www.grandforksgov.com/greenway

~ The University of North Dakota, 701.777.2011;
www.und.nodak.edu/

The trail follows the river deeper into the woods and at a place where a small sandbar had formed, I stopped to enjoy the sounds and smells of the forest and the river...

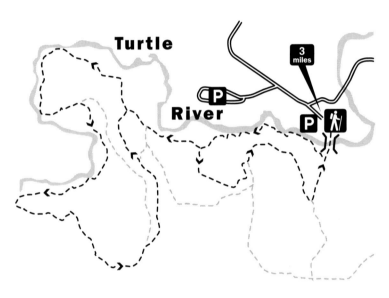

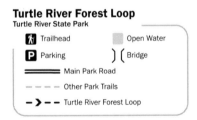

Turtle River Forest Loop
Turtle River State Park

🚶 Trailhead	▨ Open Water
🅿 Parking	) (Bridge
═══ Main Park Road	
- - - Other Park Trails	
->-- Turtle River Forest Loop	

Want to know more about this trail?
TURN TO PAGE 94

The beautiful fen on the Shady Springs Trail is filled with large trees, ferns, rushes, and springs, a perfect home for fairies or gnomes.

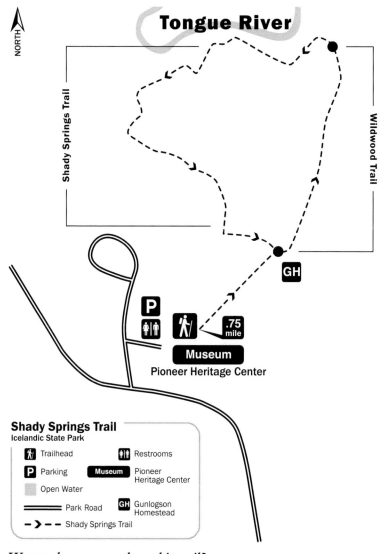

Want to know more about this trail?

TURN TO PAGE 98

As you cross the 1929 bridge, think about the barges, flatboats and steamboats that once carried passengers and freight up and down the Red River.

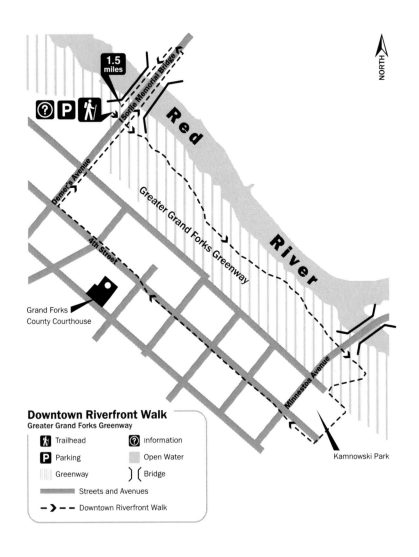

Downtown Riverfront Walk
Greater Grand Forks Greenway

🚶 Trailhead	❓ Information
🅿 Parking	▨ Open Water
▦ Greenway	) (Bridge
▬ Streets and Avenues	
– ❯ – – Downtown Riverfront Walk	

Want to know more about this trail?

TURN TO PAGE 101

MY NOTES

SIX

LAKE SAKAKAWEA

Lake Sakakawea is as immense
As the prairie around me,
Dancing in the wind
Reflecting the sky.
                    — *Susan Wefald*

AREA ATTRACTIONS

Terrific walleye fishing draws fishermen to Lake Sakakawea. Other large sport fish in the lake include northern pike, chinook salmon and small-mouth bass. Guides in the area offer guided fishing trips.

~ Sailing is a great sport on Lake Sakakawea. Exploring the many bays of the lake by canoe or motor boat is also popular. Fort Stevenson State Park has a marina with boat and canoe rentals.

~ Audubon National Wildlife Refuge features a modern visitor center, auto tour and hiking trail that entice you to explore the prairie pothole and lakeside landscape.

~ Garrison Dam National Fish Hatchery and Aquarium offers a chance to see how fish are raised before release in lakes, ponds and rivers around the state.

WHERE TO HIKE

- *Fort Stevenson State Park, Garrison*
- *Audubon National Wildlife Refuge, Coleharbor*
- *Lake Sakakawea State Park, Pick City*
- *Garrison Dam National Fish Hatchery and Aquarium, Riverdale*
- *Lewis and Clark State Park, Williston*
- *Williston Marsh Nature Area, Williston*

~ Tour a power plant at Garrison Dam and Power Plant. Some of the lowest cost electricity in the state is produced at this site.

~ Drive across Garrison Dam. With Lake Sakakawea to the north, and a beautiful section of the Missouri River Valley to the south, the views are spectacular.

~ Riverdale is worth a visit. The Army Corps of Engineers founded this charming community in the 1940s during construction of the Garrison Dam.

~ Take a scenic drive on Highway 1804, southeast of Lewis and Clark State Park. The 18-mile drive includes great views of Lake Sakakawea and surrounding rugged ranchland.

~ Golf the Links of North Dakota. This top-rated golf course overlooks Lake Sakakawea, 8 miles east of Lewis and Clark State Park.

AREA ACCOMMODATIONS

~ Fort Stevenson State Park and Lake Sakakawea State Park have pleasant campgrounds.

~ Lewis and Clark State Park has a nice campground. Seven miles east of the park there is a lake resort that offers lodging. There is also a bed and breakfast lodge nearby.

~ Garrison and Riverdale provide some options for lodging. Minot, 50 miles from Fort Stevenson State Park, and Williston, near the northern part of Lake Sakakawea, have many options for accommodations.

FORT STEVENSON STATE PARK
PURPLE CONEFLOWER TRAIL

W*hat makes this hike spectacular?* **Fort Stevenson State Park takes its name from the 19th century military fort that once stood on the Missouri River. When Lake Sakakawea was formed by Garrison Dam, this state park quickly became known as the walleye capital of North Dakota. At the trailhead is a replica of Fort Stevenson guardhouse that serves as an interpretive center for the fort and the Missouri River. Purple Coneflower Trail takes you through native prairie, where the wildflowers can be stunning, and along a bluff overlooking the lake, where – on most days – you can see Garrison Dam, six miles away.**

AT A GLANCE
PURPLE CONEFLOWER TRAIL

Map:	**Page 126**
Trail location:	**Fort Stevenson State Park**
Nearest town:	**Garrison**
Length:	**1-mile loop trail**
Elevation change:	**Less than 50 feet**
Dogs:	**Allowed on leashes**
Fees:	**Park entrance fee**
Services at trailhead:	**Interpretive center with lavatory**

DIRECTIONS TO TRAILHEAD

Fort Stevenson State Park is 3 miles south of Garrison on 41st Avenue Northwest. Trailhead parking is 1 mile south of park entrance station, near the Fort Stevenson Guardhouse Interpretive Center, which I suggest you visit at the end of the hike. To find Purple Coneflower Trail, walk down the slope from the interpretive center toward Lake Sakakawea. When you see the interpretive signs about Lewis and Clark, head east (to your left) on this trail.

SUSAN'S NOTES ON THE HIKE

It was a beautiful mid-June day when my friend Syliva joined Sandy and me on this hike. The wildflowers were in bloom, the sun was warm, there was only a slight breeze. In other words, it was a great day for hiking on an exposed prairie bluff high above the lake shore.

Be sure not to get too close to the edge of the bluff and keep a close eye on pets and small children. Bluffs along the lake are constantly eroding, creating sharp drop offs.

As you proceed along the trail, look south across the lake to Garrison Dam. Built in the 1950s to control Missouri River flooding and provide North Dakotans with a constant source of water, the dam flooded miles of forested river bottoms and completely changed the state's landscape. Many North Dakota communities, including towns in the southwestern part of the state, receive their drinking water from Lake Sakakawea.

Today, Fort Stevenson State Park is a favorite place to launch fishing expeditions. Sailing is popular too. So chances are good you'll see lots of boats on the water.

Purple Coneflower Trail takes you onto a peninsula for more great views of the big lake and a back bay. Due to the many rocks left behind around 10,000 years ago by retreating glaciers, the patch of prairie here has never been plowed. Take time to walk off the trail and look for wildflowers in the mixed-grass native prairie. In mid-June we found downy paintbrush, narrow-leaved milk-vetch and wild onion. Near the peninsula's point there's natural woody draw where we found chokecherry and buffalo berry bushes in bloom.

While we were sitting among the wildflowers on the peninsula, a white pelican flew through the sky. This is a fairly common sight in North Dakota. As many as 30,000 white pelicans nest in the state. Most nest in the Jamestown area. Pelicans without mates sometimes spend their summers on Lake Sakakawea.

As the trail loops back, you will see a weather station. Just above the small picnic area near the trail, you can choose to take a small road back to the interpretive center or cross the road and return to the trailhead via de Trobriand Loop Trail.

The de Trobriand Loop Trail takes you through a shelterbelt of trees planted to provide protection for wildlife and a buffer against the wind. Most trees in the park have been planted and watered to enable them to survive in the prairie environment.

At the end of the trail you'll return to Fort Stevenson Guardhouse Interpretive Center, which also houses an art gallery and research library. Occupied by the Army from 1867 until 1883, Fort Stevenson provided military protection for peaceful Indian tribes and served as a supply base for Fort Totten, 126 miles to the east. The rebuilt guardhouse is about two miles from the original fort site. The fort's first commander made wonderful paintings of the Missouri River Valley, which are on display in the art gallery. He painted a river valley; now we see a lake in that valley. Both are beautiful, but entirely different.

SANDY'S NOTES ON THE HIKE

On this hike I met another dog. He jumped out of the window of his owner's car in order to meet me. His owner was quite surprised when this happened. Susan's friend Sylvia joined us on this hike. She is one of my best friends.

WHAT'S FOR LUNCH?

There is a nice picnic area, with lake views, just east of Fort Stevenson Interpretive Center. Today I made chicken sandwiches at home and brought them in a cooler, along with deviled eggs, fresh peaches and pop. Sylvia brought along some delicious homemade rhubarb muffins. The town of Garrison, 3 miles north of the park, has a grocery store for picnic supplies and several restaurants.

OTHER FAVORITE HIKES

FORT STEVENSON STATE PARK
FLICKER LOOP TRAIL (2 MILES)

This pleasant, round-trip hike on the bluffs above Lake Sakakawea includes good views over the lake's western bays. The trail also gives you an opportunity to explore a woody draw at the Eagle Ridge Loop (add 0.4 mile). There is a small prairie dog town to see before turning around to make the return trip.

This section of Flicker Loop Trail starts at Fort Stevenson Interpretive Center and goes in the opposite direction of Purple Coneflower Trail. Leashed dogs are allowed.

AUDUBON NATIONAL WILDLIFE REFUGE
PRAIRIE TRAIL (1 MILE)

North Dakota has more national wildlife refuges than any other state and Audubon National Wildlife Refuge is visitor friendly. It has a modern visitor center — be sure to stop and tour the nature exhibits before or after this hike — and you can view the prairie grasslands, potholes and wildlife on foot or by taking an auto tour.

Audubon Wildlife Refuge is on Highway 83, 15 miles southeast of Garrison, near Coleharbor. Follow signs on Highway 83 to the refuge headquarters and visitor center. The trailhead is behind the visitor center. Leashed dogs are allowed.

The prairie potholes you see on this loop hike are shallow depressions on the prairie formed thousands of years ago by departing glaciers. In wet periods the potholes fill with water and provide excellent waterfowl habitat. Ducks and other waterfowl use the surrounding grasslands for nesting and may nest in the grass up to a mile from a lake or pothole.

Central North Dakota has many prairie potholes and you walk close to several on this hike. In mid June, I spotted several kinds of ducks, Canada geese, red-winged blackbirds, yellow-headed blackbirds and white-tailed deer and we stopped several times to listen to birds singing in the prairie marshes.

In the summer, refuge employees offer tours.

QUESTIONS?

～　Fort Stevenson State Park, 701.337.5576, www.parkrec.nd.gov/parks/fssp.htm

～　Audubon National Wildlife Refuge, 701.442.5474, www.fws.gov/audubon/

LAKE SAKAKAWEA STATE PARK
SANDY'S LOOP

What *makes this hike spectacular?* Lake Sakakawea, the third largest manmade lake in the country, spreads out for more than 200 miles on the old Missouri River Valley. Sandy's Loop, a combination of four scenic trails in Lake Sakakawea State Park, provides tremendous views of the lake and Garrison Dam from native prairie bluffs. A special feature on the hike is a section of eroded hillside where you can view large pieces of petrified wood, layers of lignite coal and scoria. Sections of this hike are part of 4,600-mile North Country National Scenic Trail.

AT A GLANCE

SANDY'S LOOP

Map:	Page 127
Location:	Lake Sakakawea State Park
Nearest town:	Pick City
Length:	2.5 mile loop
Elevation change:	75 feet
Dogs:	Allowed on leashes
Fees:	Park entrance fee
Services at trailhead:	Park office with lavatory

DIRECTIONS TO TRAILHEAD

Lake Sakakawea State Park is 1 mile north of Pick City. Parking for the trailhead is next to the entrance station. Sandy's Loop includes scenic segments of four trails: North Country, Overlook, Whitetail and Shoreline. Just south of the park office there is a large sign for North Country Trail. This is the start of Sandy's Loop.

SUSAN'S NOTES ON THE HIKE

Sandy's Loop begins at the terminus of North Country National Scenic Trail. All trail segments called North Country Trail are a part of the national scenic trail, which starts in New York. It's a good hike to take on a summer day because some sections are shaded by trees.

The first part of the hike on North Country Trail is through recreated prairie grasslands. It takes many years to recreate prairie grassland. Mixed-grass native prairie is made up of dozens of different grasses, forbs (wildflowers) and shrubs, while a planted prairie may at first contain only 10 or 15 different types of plants. Gradually, with grazing or burning, and with new seeds deposited by wind or wildlife, the recreated prairie becomes more diverse.

Try to spot native prairie when you switch to the Overlook Trail. One way to identify sections of native prairie is to look for rocks in the soil. Generally, in areas that have been plowed, rocks have been removed. In early July, Sandy and I passed numerous wildflowers blooming along the trail including blue flax, common yarrow and bluebells.

When we reached the resting bench on Overlook Trail, we had an excellent view of the lake and a marshy area along the lakeshore, which dries up when the lake level is low. Between drought years and wet years, water levels in the lake can vary up to 40 feet. Most of the water in Lake Sakakawea comes from Montana rivers that start high in the mountains and flow into the Missouri.

Continuing on White-Tail Trail, proceed uphill to another grand view of the park, lake and Garrison Dam. The hydroelectric power station connected with the dam produces low-cost electricity for the region. The dam itself is huge and the large facility on the west side of the dam is the intake facility for electric generation. At the top of this hill you'll find western snowberry, silver buffalo berry shrubs and little bluestem grass.

Soon the hike connects with North Country Trail. As we hiked through prairie and woody draws, Sandy and I saw a ring-necked pheasant, two white-tailed deer and two white pelicans and we enjoyed listening to birds singing in the trees.

After hiking 0.5 mile on North Country Trail, turn north on Shoreline Trail. The trails are clearly marked. In 0.33 mile you will see an eroded cliff. This small area of badlands topography reveals much about ancient history in the region.

Look for pieces of gray, petrified wood protruding from the cliff; millions of years ago – when North Dakota's climate was warm and wet – these rocks were living trees. The small black seam in the cliff is lignite coal, which is burned in North Dakota to provide electricity in the region. The layer of red clinker, known as scoria, began as clay, which was baked when the coal seams caught fire. In western North Dakota, scoria often is used to surface dirt roads.

In a short distance you again join North Country Trail. As you complete your hike, look across Lake Sakakawea and you may see the two water towers that mark the site of Riverdale, a town founded by the Corps of Engineers in the 1940s during construction of Garrison Dam. Stay on this trail back to the trailhead.

SANDY'S NOTES ON THE HIKE

Susan and I took this hike on a hot day. Towards the end of the hike, my favorite part was laying in the shade of the chokecherry trees in the woody draws. Later, Susan filled my water dish at the faucet outside the park office and I laid in the shade while she talked with the park staff.

WHAT'S FOR LUNCH?

Sandy and I found two picnic tables in a shady area adjoining the beach and I brought out my packed lunch: a roast-beef-lettuce-tomato wrap, corn chips, fresh cherries, a biscotti and pop. Dogs are not allowed on the beach or in the water in this area, so Sandy stayed on the grass while I took a swim, which felt great on a warm July day.

ANOTHER FAVORITE HIKE

GARRISON DAM NATIONAL FISH HATCHERY WETLANDS OBSERVATION TRAIL (1.5 MILE)

This loop trail offers a chance to explore a beautiful section of Missouri River shoreline and adjoining wetlands. In this area the Missouri River features high cliffs on the western bank, which you can see from the trail. On the day Sandy and I visited, we scrambled down a sandy bank and walked the sand beach for 0.25 mile along the river. The final portion of the hike features Missouri River forest, some restored prairie and interpretive signs about the Lewis and Clark Expedition in 1804-06.

To find the trailhead, from Riverdale, go west on N.D. 200. Follow signs on the dam embankment to the fish hatchery, turn south. When you reach the fish hatchery, continue south on the paved road for 0.5 mile and watch for a sign that says Wildlife Viewing Area. This sign marks the entrance to a small parking area and the trailhead. At the trailhead you'll find an information sign and a trail map. Leashed dogs are allowed.

A short distance from the trailhead you encounter a Y in the trail. Turn left and follow the path along the wetlands. There is a wildlife viewing structure in this area. The trail then skirts the edge of a public campground and proceeds to the edge of the Missouri River. Look for a side path to find a place to access the river. Sandy and I really enjoyed exploring the sandy shore. The trail loops back through an open cottonwood forest.

QUESTIONS?

🐦 Lake Sakakawea State Park, 701.487.3315, www.parkrec.nd.gov/parks/fssp.htm

🐦 Garrison Dam, US Army Corps of Engineers, 701.654.7411, www.nwo.usace.army.mil/html/Lake_Proj/garrison/dam.html

🐦 Garrison Dam National Fish Hatchery, 701.654.7451, www.fws.gov/garrisondam

LEWIS AND CLARK STATE PARK
OVERLOOK TRAIL

What makes this hike spectacular? High cliffs form the shoreline of the northwest section of Lake Sakakawea. Depending on the sun's angle and brightness, the cliff faces change color. This hike provides great views of the scenic cliffs, takes you up bluffs and along the lake through native prairie and woody draws. Lewis and Clark came through this area and camped near here in 1805. At that time there was no Garrison Dam and the Missouri was a free flowing river; but Lake Sakakawea definitely has its own beauty.

AT A GLANCE

OVERLOOK TRAIL

Map:	**Page 128**
Location:	**Lewis and Clark State Park**
Nearest town:	**Williston**
Length:	**1.5 miles roundtrip**
Elevation change:	**100 feet**
Dogs:	**Allowed on leashes**
Fees:	**Park entrance fee**
Services at trailhead:	**None**

DIRECTIONS TO TRAILHEAD

From Williston, go east 16 miles on N.D. 1804 to Williams County Road 15. Turn south on County Road 15 and go 3 miles to the park entrance station. Trailhead parking is 0.5 mile southwest of the entrance station on the park access road.

SUSAN'S NOTES ON THE HIKE

Bob, Sandy and I arrived at the park on a sunny, mid-October day and as soon as we saw the dramatic cliffs or breaks along this part of Lake Sakakawea we were ready to start hiking.

Two mowed paths lead from the trailhead parking area. The one on your right leads northwest, up a small rise. Take the one on your left through the woody draw and return by the other trail. These beautiful woody draws are such special places. This one has mature green ash, chokecherry and a single, large bur oak tree. These tough bur oaks live near the old Missouri River channel all the way west to the Montana border. Bur oaks grow slowly, so the bur oak in this draw could be several hundred years old.

Proceed under the road through a pedestrian culvert (in some places, culverts like this one allow cattle to move under roadways). Walk through another woody draw and climb the bluffs to native prairie meadows. Although there were no prairie wildflowers in bloom in October, we could spot every pale purple coneflower that had bloomed, because the seed heads were still held high in the air. The distinctive yucca lily has a large silver gray seed pod that almost looks like a flower itself. The prairie has its own beauty in any season.

Soon you will come to a Y in the trail. Take the trail on your left to a resting bench, with a great view of the lake. The trail then passes through green ash and chokecherry trees before joining the other trail. (On the return, take the alternate route across the prairie.)

Following the trail up the bluffs, the views of the lake get better and better. Be sure to take the short spur trail to the right. It leads to the highest point on the hike and a resting bench. At this point you also get good views of the rugged ranch land to the west. There are many knolls with interesting shapes.

Return to the main trail and continue hiking across the prairie to a prairie pond overlook. We saw at least 50 ducks in the pond in late October.

As we hiked back to the trailhead, the sun was low in the sky. Although it was cloudy overhead, the sun turned the cliffs along the lake a brilliant gold.

SANDY'S NOTES ON THE HIKE

Seeing wildlife on a hike always makes the walk more interesting. A ring-necked pheasant flew up in front of us as we were hiking across the prairie. I walked right by an 18-inch-long smooth green snake sunning itself on a rock, but Susan and Bob stopped to check it out. The snake's only movement was its tongue moving in and out of its mouth.

WHAT'S FOR LUNCH?

We picnicked in a shelter near the lake, just east of the trailhead. We packed a cooler with hamburger patties for grilling, buns, ketchup, deli salad, fresh pears, beverages and chocolate cupcakes. If you decide not to picnic, a resort 7 miles east of the park has a restaurant.

ANOTHER FAVORITE HIKE

WILLISTON MARSH NATURE AREA
RECREATION TRAIL (14 MILES)

If you are ready to stretch your legs and take a long hike, this may be the place to do so. A short hike is also an option. This level, round-trip hike is on the top of a dike that stretches along the Missouri River marshes south of Williston. The dike was built as a flood control measure for Williston and the water levels in the marshes depend on the levels in Lake Sakakawea.

To find the trailhead, at the junction of N.D. 1804 and 12th Avenue East in Williston, go 1 mile south on 12th Avenue East to the parking area. The trailhead, adjacent to the office and pump station of the Army Corps of Engineers, has good information about the area. Leashed dogs are allowed.

Climb up steps from the parking area to the top of the dike and you can see over the entire marsh. Hiking west, the trail extends 7 miles through the Williston marsh. Mosquitoes may be a problem on the trail in summer months and the trail should be avoided during hunting seasons.

QUESTIONS?

~   Lewis and Clark State Park, 701.859.3071,
www.parkrec.nd.gov/parks/lcsp.htm

~   U.S. Army Corps of Engineers Williston Office,
701.572.6494

While we were sitting among the wildflowers on the peninsula, a white pelican flew through the sky. This is a fairly common sight in North Dakota.

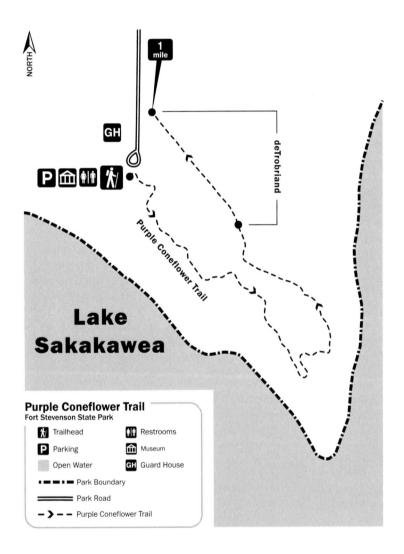

Purple Coneflower Trail
Fort Stevenson State Park

- 🚶 Trailhead
- 🅿 Parking
- ▨ Open Water
- ■-■-■ Park Boundary
- ═══ Park Road
- ->-- Purple Coneflower Trail

- 🚻 Restrooms
- 🏛 Museum
- GH Guard House

Want to know more about this trail?
TURN TO PAGE 112

Continuing on White-Tail Trail, proceed uphill to another grand view of the park, lake, and Garrison Dam.

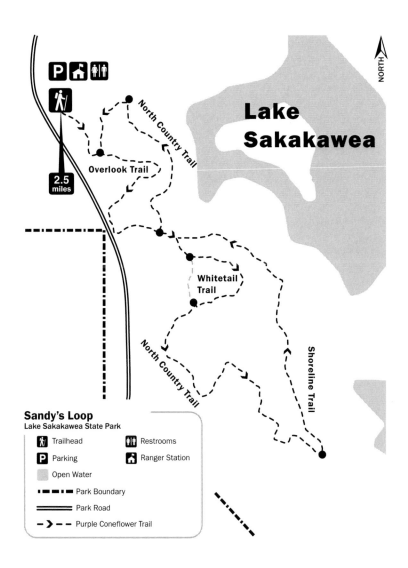

Lake Sakakawea

North Country Trail

Overlook Trail

Whitetail Trail

North Country Trail

Shoreline Trail

2.5 miles

Sandy's Loop
Lake Sakakawea State Park

🏃 Trailhead	👫 Restrooms
🅿 Parking	🏠 Ranger Station
Open Water	
■ ■ ■ ■ Park Boundary	
═══ Park Road	
➤ Purple Coneflower Trail	

Want to know more about this trail?
TURN TO PAGE 117

These beautiful woody draws are such special places. This one has mature green ash, chokecherry and a single, large bur oak tree.

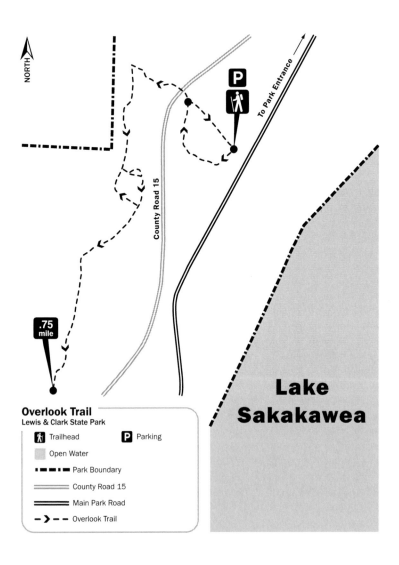

Overlook Trail
Lewis & Clark State Park

🚶 Trailhead   **P** Parking

⬛ Open Water

■ ■ ■ ■ Park Boundary

═══════ County Road 15

━━━━━━ Main Park Road

– ❯ – – Overlook Trail

Want to know more about this trail?

TURN TO PAGE 121

MY NOTES

MY NOTES

CONFLUENCE OF MISSOURI & YELLOWSTONE RIVERS

Crossing the bridge
Entering the dark tunnel,
Mysterious darkness surrounds me
And my heart flutters with excitement.
— Susan Wefald

AREA ATTRACTIONS

Sundheim Park Recreation Area provides public access to the Yellowstone River. This pleasant, river-bottom park offers a shady picnic area and a Frisbee golf course.

~ Fairview Lift Bridge, adjacent to Sundheim Park Recreation Area, was built in 1913. This historic railroad bridge is now part of a recreation trail.

~ Fort Union Trading Post National Historic Site, 22 miles southwest of Williston, once was one of the most important fur trading posts in the United States. Established on the banks of the Missouri River in 1828, the reconstructed fort is full of interesting objects from the fur-trade era.

> ### WHERE TO HIKE
>
> ● Sundheim Park Recreation Area, Fairview
>
> ● Fort Union Trading Post National Historic Site, Williston
>
> ● Missouri-Yellowstone Confluence Interpretive Center, Williston

~ Missouri-Yellowstone Confluence Interpretive Center is a modern museum and visitor center, 3 miles southeast of Fort Union Trading Post National Historic Site. Long before Lewis and Clark's Corps of Discovery visited here in 1805 and 1806, the confluence of the two rivers was an important landmark.

~ Fort Buford State Historic Site, 0.5 mile west of the Missouri-Yellowstone Confluence Interpretive Center, features several reconstructed buildings, including the house where Sitting Bull surrendered in 1881. Exhibits recreate life at a frontier military fort in the late 1800s. Visit the post cemetery where each grave provides information on the cause of a soldier's death.

~ Paddlefish snagging and snag-and-release fishing for paddlefish in North Dakota is exclusive to the Missouri River system. You'll find a public boat ramp with river access adjacent to the Missouri-Yellowstone Confluence Interpretive Center.

AREA ACCOMMODATIONS

~ Fort Buford State Historic Site offers primitive camping sites.

~ You'll find campgrounds along the Missouri River near the Missouri-Yellowstone Confluence Interpretive Center.

~ The city of Williston, 22 miles northeast, has many options for accommodations. Advance reservations are recommended.

SUNDHEIM PARK RECREATION AREA
FAIRVIEW LIFT BRIDGE AND CARTWRIGHT TUNNEL TRAIL

What makes this hike spectacular? **The combination of historic structures, exceptional scenery along the Yellowstone River and the chance to explore North Dakota's only railroad tunnel creates an unforgettable hike. Cartwright Tunnel and Fairview Lift Bridge both were completed in 1913. The panoramic view from the bridge includes tall escarpments along the river's east side and wooded banks lined with willows and massive cottonwood trees. The 0.25-mile-long tunnel is dark in the middle and a little spooky.**

DIRECTIONS TO TRAILHEAD

Sundheim Park Recreation Area is 3.5 miles east of Fairview, N.D./Mont., on Highway 200.

The trailhead is on the west side of the Yellowstone River, adjacent to Fairview Lift Bridge. There is a paved lot next to the trailhead and a parking lot near the river.

AT A GLANCE

FAIRVIEW LIFT BRIDGE
AND CARTWRIGHT TUNNEL TRAIL

Map:	**Page 140**
Location:	**Sundheim Park Recreation Area**
Nearest town:	**Fairview**
Length:	**1.2 miles roundtrip**
Elevation change:	**Less than 50 feet**
Dogs:	**Allowed on leashes**
Fees:	**None**
Services at trailhead:	**Interpretive sign, picnic tables, vault toilets**
Special note:	**Bring a flashlight to use in the tunnel**

SUSAN'S NOTES ON THE HIKE

Bob and I often have traveled along the Yellowstone River in Montana, but this was our first visit to the 17 miles of the Yellowstone River that flow through North Dakota. The river was running deep and wide on the mid-October day Bob, Sandy and I arrived at Fairview Lift Bridge.

Montana Eastern Railway began building the 1,300-foot bridge in 1912. At that time many riverboats used the Missouri and Yellowstone rivers and the government required a lift bridge be built. But, by the time the bridge was finished in 1913, shippers were no longer using riverboats and the lift was used only once.

To make the former railroad bridge safe for hikers, 4-foot-high, chain-link fences line the tracks and metal grids cover the old railroad ties. As you walk across the bridge you can see the river flowing about 50-feet beneath you. We spied like two great blue herons fishing on the riverbank.

The wide Yellowstone River Valley is fertile and the fields of sugar beets planted here reminded us of the Red River Valley's rich farmland. It's interesting to know the majority of North Dakota's sugar beets are produced in the eastern-most and western-most parts of the state.

From the bridge, you'll see yellow-colored escarpments on the eastern side of the river. These cliffs, which give the Yellowstone its name, are composed of sediment deposited 50 to 75 million years ago on an ancient flood plain. As we walked from the river's edge toward Cartwright Tunnel, we saw a large piece of petrified wood protruding from the hillside.

The tunnel opening is 23-feet wide and 24-feet tall. The walls and ceiling are completely framed in wood. The floor is dirt and the railroad tracks have been removed. Due to a slight curve, you can't see from one end of the 1,456-foot tunnel to the other. And, even thought it was a sunny morning, when we reached the middle we needed our flashlight to illuminate the way. Fortunately, aside from a few pigeons or rock doves flying about the openings, we saw no wildlife in the tunnel.

When you exit the east end of the tunnel, I recommend that you turn around and walk back to the trailhead. The trail eastward continues only a short distance and ends at private property. On the return trip, two resting benches on the bridge make nice stops.

SANDY'S NOTES ON THE HIKE

I proceeded across the bridge slowly and cautiously. Although there is a metal grid on top of the railroad ties, I could see the water far below me. When we got to the dark part of the tunnel, Susan mistook me for another animal, but we got that straightened out right away. We only saw a few pigeons in the tunnel.

WHAT'S FOR LUNCH?

For this short hike, we brought along snack bars and stopped to eat them on one of the Fairview Bridge benches. Sundheim Park Recreation Area would be a nice place to picnic. Fairview, N.D./Mont. – the town that straddles the border – is 4 miles to the west and is the closest place to pick up picnic supplies or purchase lunch.

QUESTIONS?

~ Fairview North Dakota/Montana Chamber of Commerce, 406.742.5259, www.midrivers.com/~fairview

FORT UNION TRADING POST NATIONAL HISTORIC SITE
BODMER OVERLOOK TRAIL

What makes this hike spectacular? This exceptional hike takes you to from native prairie grasslands to a hilltop overlooking the northern-most section of the Missouri River in North Dakota. You will travel to the spot where Karl Bodmer made sketches for his famous 1833 painting of the Assiniboine Indians at Fort Union Trading Post. From this vantage point you also can see Montana's historic Great Northern Railroad Snowden Lift Bridge.

AT A GLANCE

BODMER OVERLOOK TRAIL

Map:	**Page 141**
Location:	**Fort Union Trading Post National Historic Site**
Nearest town:	**Fairview**
Length:	**2 miles round trip**
Elevation change:	**130 feet**
Dogs:	**Allowed on leashes**
Fees:	**None**
Services at trailhead:	**Information sign**
Special note:	**Unprotected rail crossing on access road**

DIRECTIONS TO TRAILHEAD

Fort Union Trading Post National Historic Site is 25 miles southwest of Williston on Highway 1804. Stop at the visitor center inside the fort. The park staff will give you a trail brochure and make sure the gate to the trail-access road is unlocked. The access road, just north of the historic site entrance, crosses a railroad track. This is a main line for the Burlington Northern Santa Fe and many trains use this track, but it doesn't have crossing guards. So, be sure to stop and look up and down the track before proceeding across. You'll find a small parking lot at the trailhead.

SUSAN'S NOTES ON THE HIKE

Today, it's difficult to imagine that the fastest way to travel from Saint Louis to Fort Union Trading Post in the 1830s was a 75-day trip by steamboat. Despite the length of the journey, artists, European princes, scientists and fur traders made their way to Fort

Union on a regular basis. In 1828, the American Fur Company established Fort Union to trade European goods with area Indian tribes in exchange for fur pelts. Indians brought thousands – some years tens of thousands – of buffalo, beaver, fox, otter and other furs to the post. The fort never served as a military base.

Bob, Sandy and I took this hike on a beautiful, mid-October day, proceeding east across the native prairie on a mowed trail. Although the native grasses were no longer green, it was a good time to try identifying the dry prairie plants by their seed heads. Little blue stem grass turns a rusty pink color in the fall and we spotted large patches on the hillsides. We also saw an abundance of yucca plant, prickly pear cactus and pale purple coneflowers, stripped down to their dry cones. Old, gray fence posts strung with barbed wire and fieldstones left behind by glaciers thousands of years ago completed the fall scene.

As you climb higher on the slopes, to the west you'll see Montana's Snowden Lift Bridge. When construction began in 1912 steamboats regularly plied the river, but by the time the bridge was completed in 1913 most shipments were being made by rail and the lift portion was seldom used.

In June 1833 Swiss artist Karl Bodmer climbed these slopes to sketch Fort Union Trading Post and Assiniboine Indians, who were camping near the fort. A reproduction of his painting is displayed at Bodmer Overlook, where the valley looks much as it did in the fur-trade era. From here it's easy to imagine the Indian encampments and people conducting business around the fort.

SANDY'S NOTES ON THE HIKE

Sometimes there are cattle along this trail. Cows are big animals and they don't like dogs near their calves. To stay out of trouble when cattle are near, I walk close to Bob and Susan. If we encounter cattle near a trail, Susan and Bob clap their hands and shout and the cattle move away.

WHAT'S FOR LUNCH?

Bodmer Overlook is the perfect spot for a picnic lunch. There is a bench at the overlook and the view makes you want to linger. However, since we wanted to eat before our hike, we found a spot in the Fort Union picnic ground, adjacent to the southwest corner of the parking lot. Our fall picnic included tomato soup served hot from a thermos, salami sandwiches, crisp apples and ginger cookies. Fairview, located 10 miles south on Highway 8, is the closest place to buy picnic supplies or purchase lunch.

ANOTHER FAVORITE HIKE

MISSOURI-YELLOWSTONE CONFLUENCE INTERPRETIVE CENTER RECREATION TRAIL (0.75 MILE)

Missouri Yellowstone Confluence Interpretive Center is just 3 miles from Fort Union. For the Lewis and Clark Expedition, reaching the point where the Missouri and Yellowstone rivers meet was a major milestone. In their journals the explorers commented on the breadth of the fertile plain, the many trees and the abundance of wildlife. It continues to be a beautiful spot to visit. The 0.75-mile, round-trip trail allows you to explore an oxbow wetland near the confluence.

Missouri Yellowstone Confluence Interpretive Center is 1 mile south of Highway 1804, 22 miles southwest of Williston. You'll find the trailhead behind the visitor center. Leashed dogs are allowed.

There's no fee for entering the center or hiking the trail, but there is a fee for touring center exhibits, which I encourage you to do. The center's exit doors open onto a view of the confluence. Here the Missouri River is still free flowing and looks much as it did

200 years ago. When you are ready to move on, walk straight ahead down the paved path. Then I suggest you go left (east) on the paved path that curves up the slope toward an interpretive exhibit.

Return to the front of the visitor center and follow the 0.25-mile trail west along the prairie riverbank, adjacent to a backwater marsh. The trail crosses an historic bridge that was moved to the site. Eastern cottonwood and willow trees line the bank. And, in October, we saw hundreds of ducks and geese on the water.

QUESTIONS?

~ Fort Union Trading Post National Historic Site, 701.572.9083, www.nps.gov/fousqw

~ Missouri-Yellowstone Confluence Interpretive Center, 701.572.9034, www.nd.gov/historicsites/index.html

~ Fort Buford State Historic Site, 701.572.9034, www.nd.gov/historicsites/index.html

As you walk across the bridge, you can see the river flowing about 50 feet beneath you.

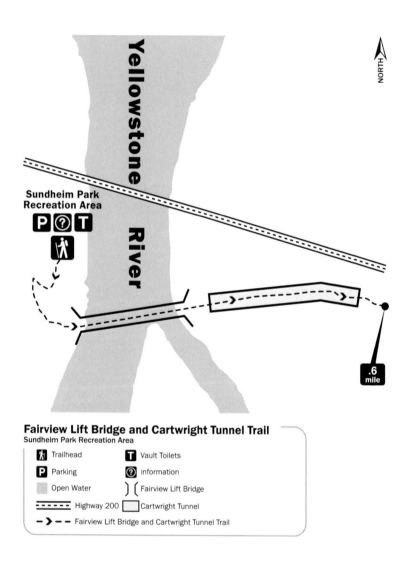

Fairview Lift Bridge and Cartwright Tunnel Trail
Sundheim Park Recreation Area

🚶 Trailhead		🅣 Vault Toilets	
🅟 Parking		ⓘ Information	
Open Water		) (Fairview Lift Bridge	
▪▪▪▪▪ Highway 200		☐ Cartwright Tunnel	
— ❯ — — Fairview Lift Bridge and Cartwright Tunnel Trail			

Want to know more about this trail?
TURN TO PAGE 132

Little blue stem grass turns a rusty pink color in the fall and we spotted large patches of it on the hillsides.

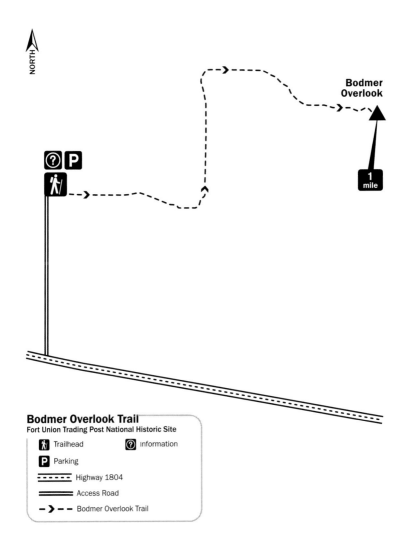

Want to know more about this trail?

TURN TO PAGE 135

MY NOTES

- EIGHT -
NATIONAL WILDLIFE REFUGES
& OTHER SCENIC LOCATIONS

Seeking out a quiet place
I find quacking ducks,
Honking geese, singing birds.
I revel in the noisy silence.
> — Susan Wefald

AREA ATTRACTIONS

A ssumption Abbey and Saint Mary's Church in Richardton are open to visitors. Saint Mary's Church, built in 1906, has a gorgeous painted interior and two large towers that can be seen for miles across the prairie.

WHERE TO HIKE

- *Schnell Recreation Area, Richardton*
- *Upper Souris National Wildlife Refuge, Minot*
- *Des Lacs National Wildlife Refuge, Kenmare*
- *Lostwood National Wildlife Refuge, Stanley*

The Enchanted Highway features seven huge, scrap-metal sculptures by folk artist Gary Greff. The 32-mile highway begins about 12 miles west of Richardton at I-94/Exit 72. Turn south on the Regent-Gladstone Road. The first sculpture you'll see is the 110-foot-tall Geese in Flight.

Upper Souris National Wildlife Refuge lures visitors with a scenic drive, canoeing and hiking trails.

The Scandinavian Heritage Center and Park, Roosevelt Park Zoo and North Dakota State Fair (held in July) can all be found in Minot, 25 miles southeast of Upper Souris National Wildlife Refuge.

Des Lacs National Wildlife Refuge Scenic Drive, a national scenic backway, extends 14 miles along the wetlands of the Des Lacs Valley. The southern half of the drive offers good views of the refuge's marshes and lakes; the northern half is pleasantly shaded by trees.

Kenmare's Danish Mill is open to the public on the Town Square. Built in 1902, it's the only Danish mill in the United States.

Lake County Historical Museum, a pioneer village, is in Kenmare.

~ Lostwood National Wildlife Refuge Lookout Tower is 100 feet tall. A 50-foot viewing platform offers great views of the surrounding countryside. The refuge also has a 7-mile auto tour.

~ Oil wells are a part of the surrounding countryside near Lostwood National Wildlife Refuge. Western North Dakota is home to the Bakken and Three Forks oil shale formations, two of the richest oil shale formations in the United States.

AREA ACCOMMODATIONS

~ Schnell Recreation Area has six camping sites. Dickinson, 20 miles west, has many options for lodging. Reserve motel rooms in advance.

~ Minot, 25 miles southeast of Upper Souris National Wildlife Refuge, has many accommodation choices.

~ Kenmare, adjacent to Des Lacs National Wildlife Refuge, offers good accommodation choices. Reserve motel rooms in advance.

SCHNELL RECREATION AREA
SLATER POND AND THE BUR OAK NATURE TRAIL

What *makes this hike spectacular?* **The 2,000-acre Schnell Recreation Area was a working cattle ranch for 120 years. This hike offers grand views of surrounding ranchland. You'll also explore the north-facing slope of a ridge where a natural spring flows into a creek and then into a marsh. Another beautiful spot is the small, peaceful valley where you'll find Slater Pond. I encourage you to take your time on this trail. Pause often**

to enjoy the scenery and wildlife and to think about the ranchers and others who have loved this land for generations. This is truly an oasis on the prairie.

AT A GLANCE

SLATER POND AND
THE BUR OAK NATURE TRAIL

Map:	**Page 161**
Location:	**Schnell Recreation Area**
Nearest town:	**Richardton**
Length:	**3.5-mile loop**
Elevation change:	**240 feet**
Dogs:	**Allowed on leashes**
Fees:	**None**
Services at trailhead:	**None**
Hunting alert:	**Avoid hiking here during hunting seasons**

DIRECTIONS TO TRAILHEAD

Schnell Recreation Area is 3 miles northeast of Richardton. Exit Interstate 94 at Exit 84. To find the trailhead, drive 0.75 mile north of I-94 to Highway 10. Turn right and go 1 mile east and then turn left and go 0.5 mile north. Look for a small parking area on your right. The trailhead is marked with a sign: Slater Pond 0.5 mile. This 3.5-mile loop hike includes four trails: Grassland, Connecting, Bur Oak Trail and Woodland. Start the hike on Grassland Trail.

SUSAN'S NOTES ON THE HIKE

Looking northeast from Grassland Trail, you can see for miles across the surrounding prairie. It's fun to imagine what this place might have been like during its long history as a cattle ranch. The ranch became public property in 1993 through a joint effort by the

Bureau of Land Management, the Conservation Fund, the Richard King Mellon Foundation and the Schnell family, which owned the ranch for 80 years.

As you proceed down into the small valley to Slater Pond, you will pass through wooded areas including bur oak, green ash and chokecherry trees. When Sandy and I visited the pond in mid May, turtles were sunning themselves on the logs in the pond. Fishing is allowed, so bring your fishing license and your pole.

Cross Slater Pond dam on Connecting Trail and continue east along a wooded, dry creek bed for 0.5 mile toward Bur Oak Nature Trail. Sandy and I saw much wildlife on this section of the trail: ring-necked pheasants peeking through the tall grass, mule deer grazing on a hill and birds singing in the trees.

When you reach Bur Oak Nature Trail, go to your right. This beautiful section of the trail takes you near a spring-fed marsh. As you proceed you'll find interpretive signs, a natural spring, little bridges crossing a small creek and many opportunities to see waterfowl.

The trail circles back to a small picnic area next to another pond. There is a lavatory here and more information about Schnell Recreation Area. This is an excellent place to stop and eat a picnic lunch.

Continue along the north side of the marsh on Bur Oak Nature Trail for about 0.5 mile, take Connecting Trail that returns to Slater Pond and then take Woodland Trail back to the trailhead. As you go up the wooded ridge, be sure to turn around and look at the beautiful views of the pond and distant ranchland.

SANDY'S NOTES ON THE HIKE

My nose kept busy smelling all the ring-necked pheasants and waterfowl. I drank water at Slater Pond while eyeing the turtles sunning on the logs. Susan put tick repellent on me before the hike. In May and early June, tick repellent really helps keep those ticks away.

WHAT'S FOR LUNCH?

In addition to the designated picnic area at the start of the Bur Oak Nature Trail, this hike has many perfect picnic spots (without tables). I chose to eat my purchased subway sandwich, chips and an apple at Slater Pond. I don't know if it was the warm spring day, the scenery or the food, but it was great lunch. Dickinson, 20 miles west, has numerous places to buy picnic supplies or purchase lunch.

OTHER HIKES IN THE RECREATION AREA

All of Schnell Recreation Area is open to cross country hiking. Head off across the prairie and climb a small rise to make your own discoveries.

QUESTIONS?

～ Schnell Recreation Area, 701.227.7700; www.blm.gov/mt/st/en/fo/north/_dakota_field/schnell.html

UPPER SOURIS NATIONAL WILDLIFE REFUGE
COTTONWOOD NATURE TRAIL

What makes this hike spectacular? Cottonwood Nature Trail offers scenic views of the Upper Souris River Valley. The Souris River flows south from Canada into North Dakota and then turns north and flows back into Canada, contributing its waters to Hudson Bay. The hike takes you up native mixed-grass prairie slopes for terrific views of Lake Darling and the Upper Souris River and down through a wooded coulee. Wildlife is abundant here so be sure to bring your binoculars.

AT A GLANCE

COTTONWOOD NATURE TRAIL

Map:	**Page 162**
Location:	**Upper Souris National Wildlife Refuge**
Nearest town:	**Minot**
Length:	**1-mile loop**
Elevation change:	**100 feet**
Dogs:	**Allowed on leashes**
Fees:	**None**
Services at trailhead:	**None**
Special note:	**Trails closed during deer hunting season and planned burns**

DIRECTIONS TO TRAILHEAD

Souris National Wildlife Refuge is 25 miles northwest of Minot on Ward County Road 6. You'll find the trailhead at interpretive sign No. 8 on Prairie Marsh Scenic Drive. The 3-mile scenic drive, on the west side of the Souris River, has interpretive signs and platforms for viewing wildlife.

SUSAN'S NOTES ON THE HIKE

Since this is the Cottonwood Trail, I expected to hike among eastern cottonwood trees, however, the only cottonwoods along this trail are those the Civilian Conservation Corps planted near the trail parking area in the 1930s.

The trail immediately goes up the slopes above the Souris River. And while the mixed-grass native prairie deserves your full attention, be sure to take time to turn around and look at the valley behind you. The wide valley was formed about 12,000 years ago by large releases of meltwater during the Wisconsin Glacial Episode. Lake Darling was formed in the 1930s by damming the river. South of the dam, the river follows its natural, wooded channel to the southeast.

When Sandy and I hiked this trail in late April, the prairie was just turning green. We saw light purple pasque flowers, or prairie crocus, pushing through last year's brown prairie grasses. Thousands of ants were scrambling on a large anthill near the trail, all of the shrubs and trees were budding and geese were honking in the distance. As we hiked up the prairie slope we surprised a pair of pheasants. Wild turkeys also frequent the area.

After about 0.5 mile, the trail curves down beside and then through a long, narrow wooded valley called a coulee. Named by early French hunters and traders, coulees in this area are filled with green ash and box elder trees. We spotted shelf fungus growing on tree trunks and two deer.

The trail leads out of the coulee up a steep prairie slope to a prairie ridge. On the day of our hike, refuge officials were burning part of the native prairie. Fires started by lightning strikes once were a normal part of prairie life. Today fire is an important land-management tool for controlling the spread of shrubs and non-native grasses, such as brome and Kentucky blue grass, and keeping native prairies healthy.

The last 0.33 mile of the trail leads downhill through mixed-grass prairie slopes to the parking area. Exploring just a small section of this beautiful valley makes you want to spend more time here. Cross-country hiking is allowed in this part of the refuge.

SANDY'S NOTES ON THE HIKE

Susan was surprised that leashed dogs are allowed on the refuge trails and told me to be on my best behavior. I perked up when the pheasants flew up right in front of us, but I must admit my most interesting adventure of the day was finding and sniffing a painted turtle on Oxbow Nature Trail. Ticks already were out in late April, but I was prepared with tick repellent.

WHAT'S FOR LUNCH?

I ate lunch at Lake Darling Landing No. 1, which is equipped with a picnic table, a vault toilet and a nice view of the lake. Since asparagus is abundant in late April, I brought along fresh-cooked asparagus spears, red leaf lettuce, hardboiled eggs, my favorite dressing and combined these ingredients into a salad. A buttered roll, beverage and an oatmeal-chocolate-chip cookie completed my meal. You'll find another nice picnic site near the trailhead for Oxbow Nature Trail.

ANOTHER FAVORITE HIKE

UPPER SOURIS NATIONAL WILDLIFE REFUGE
OXBOW NATURE TRAIL (1 MILE)

This interpretive, 1-mile loop trail follows the edge of an oxbow pond, formed when the river changed its course. The area is lightly wooded with green ash trees. In late April we identified several types of ducks and other waterfowl in marshes along the trail.

The trailhead for Oxbow Nature Trail is in Outlet Fishing Area. The road to the fishing area is near the refuge headquarters and across the road from an old lookout tower. In addition to the trailhead, you'll find a fishing pier, parking lot, picnic tables and a vault toilet. Fishing is allowed, so bring your pole and fishing license and try your luck. There is a map at the trailhead. Leashed dogs are allowed.

After walking through a lightly wooded area for 0.25 mile, the 1-mile trail winds through a sunny, floodplain meadow with distant views of the valley's prairie slopes. At one point near the oxbow pond you'll see marsh grass that's more than 10 feet high. Sandy found a 6-inch-long painted turtle in the grass. I carefully picked up the turtle and turned it over to admire the beautiful red, brown, yellow and green design on its bottom shell. The colorful design reminded me of a stunning modern painting.

QUESTIONS?

～ Upper Souris National Wildlife Refuge, 701.468.5467, www.fws.gov/uppersouris

DES LACS NATIONAL WILDLIFE REFUGE
MUNCH'S COULEE NATURE TRAIL

What makes this hike spectacular? **Des Lacs National Wildlife Refuge, designated by the American Bird Conservancy as a globally important bird area, encompasses three long lakes and interconnecting marshes, which provide excellent habitat for migratory and nesting waterfowl. Centered by Des Lacs Valley, the refuge also has many side valleys, or coulees. Munch's Coulee Nature Trail takes you near wetlands, up a woody draw and across prairie slopes to outstanding views of the valley.**

AT A GLANCE
MUNCH'S COULEE NATURE TRAIL

Map:	**Page 163**
Location:	**Des Lacs National Wildlife Refuge**
Nearest town:	**Kenmare**
Length:	**1-mile loop**
Elevation change:	**115 feet**
Dogs:	**Allowed on leashes**
Fees:	**None**
Services at trailhead:	**Interpretive sign with map of trail**
Special note:	**No winter maintenance on road to trailhead**

DIRECTIONS TO TRAILHEAD

Munch's Coulee Nature Trail is 5 miles south of Kenmare on Des Lacs National Wildlife Refuge Scenic Drive. Munch's Coulee is well marked and the trailhead is adjacent to the road on the south end of the refuge. The scenic drive isn't maintained in the winter, so if you plan an off-season visit be sure to contact refuge headquarters for road conditions.

SUSAN'S NOTES ON THE HIKE

Hundreds of species of waterfowl and wetland birds use Des Lacs Valley and surrounding refuge for breeding and migration habitat. In my car travels across North Dakota, I have whizzed past countless prairie wetlands, so it was great to slow down and identify the ducks, geese and grebes that live here.

Des Lacs Valley is at the center of 19,500-acre Des Lacs National Wildlife Refuge. Shaped 10,000 years ago by the sudden release of water from a glacial meltwater lake, the valley is about 0.75 miles wide and – in some places – 165 feet deep. You can't see the valley from a distance, because its prairie slopes and U-shaped side valleys drop below the level, surrounding farmland.

My nephew John, Sandy and I began our morning hike by observing several ducks swimming in a small wetland near the trailhead. Based on the pamphlet we brought with us, we identified the ducks as blue-winged teal.

The first 0.25 mile of the trail is paved and leads to a bench where you can sit and enjoy the sounds of a marsh and the view of south-facing prairie slope. In mid-May, the wild plum and juneberry bushes were in bloom in the thickets along the trail at the bottom of the coulee.

To continue on the 1-mile hike, backtrack a short distance and take the mowed path leading up the coulee slope. You'll find another bench at the top of the hill overlooking lower Des Lacs Lake. The hike continues along woodlands that are dominated by green ash, with an understory of chokecherry and other tall shrubs, and through native prairie grasslands, where cool-season grasses were beginning to grow and a few wildflowers were in bloom.

At the western-most point of the hike, there is a terrific view of Middle and Lower Des Lacs lakes and their connecting marshes. During our spring visit, green ash trees on the valley's north-facing slope were just beginning to leaf, the sky was filled with ducks and geese, and the wind blended the sweet smell of blossoming trees with the songs of prairie birds.

As the trail loops back to the parking lot, it proceeds down the prairie slope facing Lower Des Lacs Lake. Using binoculars to scan the valley wetlands below, we spotted canvasbacks, redheads and ruddy ducks, Canada geese and several species of grebes. Many are colorful, but the ruddy duck was my favorite.

SANDY'S NOTES ON THE HIKE

At several points on this trail I had to sit still while John and Susan took time to identify ducks and other waterfowl. Sometimes, I like to chase Canada geese, but this was not the time or place for that type of adventure.

WHAT'S FOR LUNCH?

Any of the three benches along this hike make perfect picnic spots, but today we decided to eat in Kenmare's town square park. This pleasant park has a Danish windmill, large shade trees and is across the street from an old-time soda fountain. For today's lunch we enjoyed pastrami on rye sandwiches, cold slaw and dill pickles and bought ice cream treats for dessert. Kenmare has several restaurants and also a grocery store to purchase picnic supplies.

Another beautiful picnic area is at Tasker's Coulee, 2 miles south of the refuge headquarters. The wooded picnic area includes a stone picnic shelter with fireplace, picnic tables, grills, restrooms and short trails that wind through the coulee bottom. The Civilian Conservation Corps built the picnic shelter from native stone in the 1930s. Contact refuge headquarters for information about seasonal opening and closing dates.

OTHER HIKES IN THE REFUGE

A number of service roads on the wildlife refuge are limited to foot traffic. Some allow close access to the marshes and lakes in the valley. However, when viewing waterfowl, your car often acts as a blind and you may have better luck seeing waterfowl from within your car than outside your car.

QUESTIONS?

~ Des Lacs National Wildlife Refuge, 701.385.4046, www.fws.gov/jclarksalyer/deslacs/

LOSTWOOD NATIONAL WILDLIFE REFUGE
NATURE TRAIL

What makes this hike spectacular? If you want to experience miles of pristine native northern mixed grass prairie, take this hike. The expansive views across the prairie extend for miles in all directions. You also get a chance to view, up close, some of the most productive waterfowl habitat in the world. The 26,900-acre Lostwood National Wildlife Refuge is in the Missouri Coteau region. Coteau means small hills in French. This nature trail winds among these small prairie hills interspersed with prairie potholes, where waterfowl and other wetland species live and breed. Here at Lostwood, you really get a feeling for what the vast prairies were like before settlement occurred.

DIRECTIONS TO TRAILHEAD

Lostwood National Wildlife Refuge is 22 miles north of Stanley. The trailhead is on the scenic drive, 1.8 miles west of refuge headquarters. Be sure to stop at the refuge headquarters to pick up informational pamphlets on the refuge and the auto tour. You'll also find lavatories here. The trailhead is at marker No. 2 on the auto tour.

AT A GLANCE

NATURE TRAIL

Map:	**Page 164**
Location:	**Lostwood National Wildlife Refuge**
Nearest town:	**Stanley**
Length:	**7.4-mile loop**
Elevation change:	**300 feet**
Dogs:	**Allowed on leashes**
Fees:	**None**
Services at trailhead:	**None**
Special note:	**Trail closed October through April**

SUSAN'S NOTES ON THE HIKE

My nephew John, Sandy and I loved hiking the native northern mixed-grass prairies of Lostwood National Wildlife Refuge. The vastness of the prairie is overwhelming, with expansive views of rolling hills that stretch from horizon to horizon.

The trail is marked with small brown signs bearing the image of a hiker. There is no shade, so in hot weather plan to hike in early morning or in the evening. Bring plenty of water for you and your pet. For a shorter hike, hike 1 mile west, to where the trail turns south, and then turn around and retrace your steps to the trailhead.

In mid May, the sky was clear blue, the breeze was light and the temperature was moderate. John and I slathered on sunscreen and hiked west on the grassy trail. The first mile of the trail runs between national refuge land (on the left) and 5,577 acres of refuge land that's been designated a national wilderness area (on the right). To the untrained eye, they look the same.

The small hills here were formed thousands of years ago when the Wisconsin glacier receded, leaving behind a huge ridge of sand

and gravel called a moraine. As large chunks of glacial ice broke off and melted within the moraine, small wetlands known as prairie potholes or sloughs were formed. Potholes are common on North Dakota's prairies – this refuge alone has 2,000 wetland areas – but potholes in the Missouri Coteau are deeper and more permanent. In fact, the Missouri Coteau is recognized as one of the most productive areas in the world for breeding waterfowl.

The first pothole we passed on our hike, edged by a few quaking aspen trees, was populated by several species of ducks, including canvasbacks and northern shovelers. A pothole never stops creating good habitat. A dry pothole breaks down plant material, just waiting for wet conditions again.

In the distance we could see cattle grazing. Because grazing encourages plants to develop stronger root systems, cattle are an important part of maintaining a healthy prairie. Before cattle, bison were part of this natural cycle. I was pleased to see a western meadowlark perched on a fence post, singing its cheerful song. North Dakota's state bird is a ground-nesting bird and needs prairie habitat to survive.

Turning south, the trail goes up and down small prairie slopes. Stopping to take a close look at a section of native prairie, we noticed how thick and tough the sod felt under our feet. In order to grow here, plants must withstand major temperature changes, draught, wind, fire and grazing. Seeds from prairie plants first grow roots deep into the soil; the top growth appears much later. Those deep roots provide moisture during dry years and protection from prairie fires.

Many of the more than 750 species of plants in the refuge are wildflowers or forbs. Domestic varieties of these wildflowers, such as penstemon and pale purple coneflower, are great for perennial flowerbeds, because they are winter hardy and tolerate draught. In mid May, I spied a clump of purple violets pushing through the thick thatch. We also saw at least five different yellow wildflowers, including prairie golden pea, in bloom.

At the marker indicating the trail's turn to the east, John, Sandy and I stopped to rest. In the distance, we could see Upper Lostwood

Lake. In the west, we could see blackened areas of the prairie refuge that recently had been burned. Controlled burns keep the prairie intact by reducing the number of quaking aspen trees and preventing the spread of woody shrubs. Hawks like living in prairie trees and kill many songbirds, so when tree growth is kept in check prairie songbirds are more likely to survive.

Near School Section Lake the hiking trail joins the route of the refuge auto tour. This is the only hike in this book that follows a trail that allows motorized vehicles, but traffic here is generally light and on our hike we didn't encounter any vehicles.

At School Section Lake and an adjacent slough we used binoculars to try to identify ducks, geese, shorebirds and freshwater divers, like grebes, as they moved about the water. I'm convinced I saw a marbled godwit, a shorebird that nests on the prairie, but John wasn't so sure. Distinguishing prairie songbirds was even more difficult, as they all seem to share the same color palette of brown, white and beige. However, we both agreed it was a mule deer we saw bounding across the prairie and – at trail marker No. 8 – we saw a moose.

We had stopped to eat lunch at marker No. 8 and had spent about 30 minutes resting and talking, when a moose trotted out from behind a prairie hill. It was only about 300 yards away and headed for a small pothole. We watched the moose walk into the trees at the water's edge, wade into the water and begin munching on its own lunch.

From School Section Lake, the hike back on the auto tour/trail is mainly uphill. As you go, be sure to turn around occasionally and look at the view behind you.

SANDY'S NOTES ON THE HIKE

There are metal cattle guards located along the trail. I wasn't sure I wanted to cross the first one, but there was no way around it. So, Susan crossed with me, coaxing me along, and John called me from the other side. My paws slipped between the slats the first time, but at the second cattle guard, I carefully placed my paws on each slat and was across in no time.

WHAT'S FOR LUNCH?

We ate at marker No. 8, but there are many lovely spots for a picnic along the trail. Today's lunch included canned salmon (we remembered a can opener), crackers, sliced cucumbers, cherry tomatoes and cheese. We also brought along bar cookies and apples for dessert. Stanley, 22 miles south, is the nearest town to purchase picnic supplies so plan carefully.

OTHER HIKES IN THE REFUGE

Cross-country hiking is allowed in the national wilderness area. For special regulations regarding this area, contact the refuge office.

QUESTIONS?

~ Lostwood National Wildlife Refuge, 701.848.2722, www.fws.gov/lostwood/lostwoodnwr.htm

When Sandy and I visited the pond in mid May, turtles were sunning themselves on the logs in the pond.

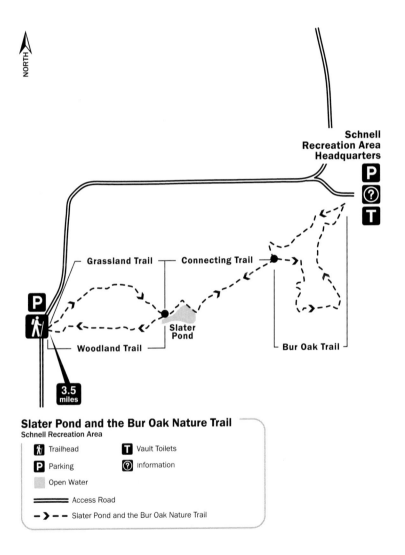

Slater Pond and the Bur Oak Nature Trail
Schnell Recreation Area

- 🚶 Trailhead
- 🅿 Parking
- ▪ Open Water
- ══ Access Road
- ➤ Slater Pond and the Bur Oak Nature Trail
- T Vault Toilets
- ❓ Information

Want to know more about this trail?
TURN TO PAGE 145

And while the mixed-grass native prairie deserves your full attention, be sure to take time to turn around and look at the valley behind you.

Marsh along Souris River

Cottonwood Nature Trail
Upper Souris National Wildlife Refuge

🚶 Trailhead	🅿 Parking
Open Water	
══════ Prairie Marsh Scenic Drive	
– › – – Cottonwood Nature Trail	

Want to know more about this trail?
TURN TO PAGE 148

Using binoculars to scan the valley wetlands below, we spotted canvasbacks, redheads and ruddy ducks, Canada geese and several species of grebes.

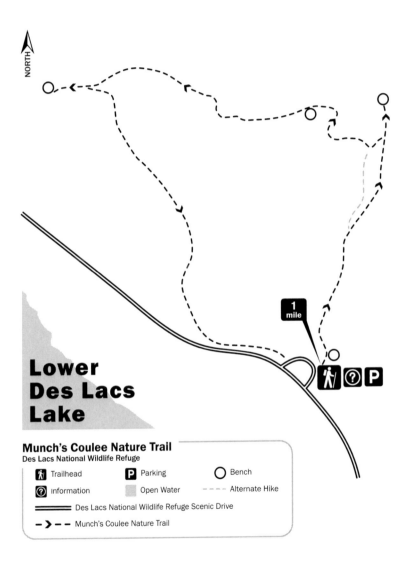

Lower Des Lacs Lake

Munch's Coulee Nature Trail
Des Lacs National Wildlife Refuge

| 🚶 Trailhead | 🅿 Parking | ⭕ Bench |
| 🛈 Information | Open Water | – – – Alternate Hike |

═══ Des Lacs National Wildlife Refuge Scenic Drive

–ᐳ– – Munch's Coulee Nature Trail

Want to know more about this trail?
TURN TO PAGE 152

In fact, the Missouri Coteau is recognized as one of the most productive areas in the world for breeding waterfowl.

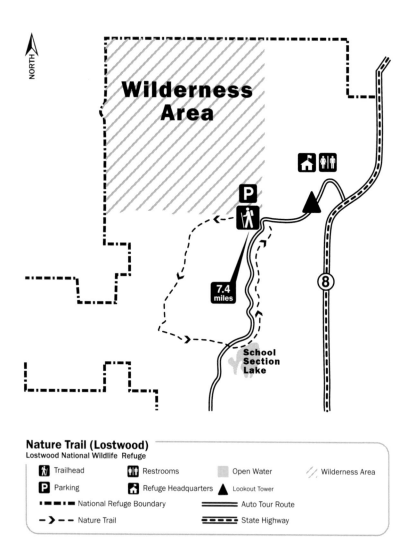

Nature Trail (Lostwood)
Lostwood National Wildlife Refuge

Trailhead	Restrooms	Open Water	Wilderness Area
Parking	Refuge Headquarters	Lookout Tower	
National Refuge Boundary		Auto Tour Route	
Nature Trail		State Highway	

Want to know more about this trail?

TURN TO PAGE 156

MY NOTES

HIKES AT A GLANCE

DOGS NOT ALLOWED
Prairie Trail **15**
The Labyrinth Walk **16**
Painted Canyon Trail **62**
Painted Canyon Nature Trail **66**
Trail to Sperati Point **81**
Shady Springs Trail **98**
Settlers Trail **100**

HIKES WITH BISON PRESENT
Prairie Trail **15**
Painted Canyon Trail **62**
Painted Canyon Nature Trail **66**
Trail to Sperati Point **81**

HIKES WITHIN 10 MILES OF INTERSTATE 94 (FROM EAST TO WEST)
Sageway Path and the Labyrinth Walk **16**
Sibley Nature Park Trail **19**
Missouri Valley Legacy Trail **8**
Sertoma Riverside Park Zoo Loop **10**
Double Ditch State Historic Site Interpretive Trail **11**
Missouri River Natural Area Trail **7**
Little Soldier Loop Trail **3**
Fort Abraham Lincoln Recreation Trail **6**
Slater Pond and the Bur Oak Nature Trail **145**
Painted Canyon Trail **62**
Painted Canyon Nature Trail **66**

HIKES WITHIN 15 MILES OF HIGHWAY 2 (FROM EAST TO WEST)
Downtown Riverfront Walk **101**
University of North Dakota Campus Walk **104**
Turtle River Forest Loop **94**
Lostwood National Wildlife Refuge Nature Trail **156**
Williston Marsh Nature Area Recreation Trail **124**
Missouri Yellowstone Confluence Interpretive Center Recreation Trail **138**
Bodmer Overlook Trail **135**

HIKES WITH HUNTING ALERTS

Black Lake Trail in Strawberry Lake Recreation Area   **36**
Mineral Spring and Waterfall trail   **49**
Oak Ridge Hiking Trail   **52**
Hike to Iron Springs   **52**
Summit Trail   **71**
Bennett Trail   **74**
Kate's Walk on the Maah Daah Hey Trail   **77**
Williston Marsh Nature Area Recreation Trail   **124**
Slater Pond and the Bur Oak Nature Trail   **145**

HIKES OF 1 MILE OR LESS

Double Ditch State Historic Site Interpretive Trail   **11**
Sibley Nature Park Trail   **19**
Hike to Butte Saint Paul   **31**
Little Twig Nature Trail   **48**
Painted Canyon Nature Trail – **66**
Shady Springs Trail   **98**
University of North Dakota Campus Walk   **104**
Purple Coneflower Trail   **112**
Audubon National Wildlife Refuge Prairie Trail   **116**
Missouri Yellowstone Confluence Interpretive
   Center Recreation Trail   **138**
Cottonwood Nature Trail   **148**
Oxbow Nature Trail   **151**
Munch's Coulee Nature Trail   **152**

HIKES OF 1.2 TO 2.5 MILES

Little Soldier Loop Trail   **3**
Fort Abraham State Park Recreation Trail   **6**
Sertoma Riverside Park Zoo Loop   **10**
Upper Loop of the Ma-a-koti Trail   **12**
The Nature Conservancy Cross Ranch Preserve Prairie Trail   **15**
Sageway Path and Labyrinth Walk   **16**
Old Oak Trail   **30**
Formal Gardens Border Walk   **33**
Lakeview Hiking Trail   **35**
Valley View Trail   **46**
Oak Ridge Hiking Trail   **52**

Travois Trail **70**
Trail to Sperati Point **81**
Downtown Riverfront Walk **101**
Flicker Loop Trail **115**
Sandy's Loop **117**
Wetlands Observation Trail **120**
Overlook Trail **121**
Fairview Lift Bridge and Cartwright Tunnel Trail **132**
Bodmer Overlook Trail **135**

HIKES OF 3 TO 4 MILES
Missouri Valley Legacy Trail **8**
Kings Highway Trail **27**
Black Lake Trail **36**
Mineral Springs and Waterfall Trail **49**
Painted Canyon Trail **62**
Bennett Trail **74**
Kate's Walk on the Maah Daah Hey Trail **77**
Turtle River Forest Loop **94**
Settlers Trail **100**
Slater Pond and the Bur Oak Nature Trail **145**

HIKES LONGER THAN 5 MILES
Missouri River Natural Area Trail **7**
Two Rivers Trail **15**
Hike to Iron Springs **52**
Bob's Loop **67**
Summit Trail **71**
Williston Marsh Nature Area Recreation Trail **124**
Lostwood National Wildlife Refuge Nature Trail **156**

MY NOTES